Miracles

IN THE DARKNESS

Miracles

IN THE DARKNESS

BUILDING A LIFE
AFTER LOSS

JULIE CLUFF

CFI
An imprint of Cedar Fort, Inc.
Springville, Utah

ISBN 13: 978-1-4621-3752-7

Published by CFI, an imprint of Cedar Fort, Inc.
2373 W. 700 S., Springville, UT 84663
Distributed by Cedar Fort, Inc., www.cedarfort.com

LIBRARY OF CONGRESS CONTROL NUMBER: 2020937943

Cover design by Shawnda T. Craig
Cover design © 2020 Cedar Fort, Inc.

Printed in the United States of America

10 9 8 7 6 5 4 3 2 1

Printed on acid-free paper

Dedication

This book is dedicated to my multitude of friends and dear family who reached out to lift and love me through the darkest hours of my life. I find it impossible to fully express all my love and gratitude for you.

To my beautiful, smart, supportive, and loving children: Stephanie, Kristin, Dallin, James, Carrie, and David. I love you. You inspire me every day.

To my steady, brilliant, loving, and tender husband, who stood by me as together we bore the weight of tragedy. Where would I be without you? I love you.

Contents

Our family, Florida, 2000

INTRODUCTION

We All Have a Story

We all have a story. Every single person has an extraordinary and important story. Our distinctive experiences make us who we are.

Absolutely no two people on the planet share the same story even within the same family, which I think is so remarkable. The uniqueness in each of our lives is amazing. And to consider that our Heavenly Father knows and loves each of us in our individuality is even more astounding.

When we tell our story, we are telling how we perceived the events that shaped our life. Our perceptions are everything. We can choose to write our character in the story as the villain, the victim, or the hero, even if it's the same story.

With the perspective of time and healing, I choose to see the love and light in my story despite the moments of victimhood and villainy. But it wasn't always that way.

In the dark, desperate days and weeks following the death of my children, I saw myself only as the victim. The incessant questions in my head included, *Why did this happen? Will my life always be this painful? How will I ever survive? How can I go on living in this overwhelming anguish?*

Author Walter Anderson said, "Bad things do happen. How I respond to them defines my character and the quality of my life. But I can choose to sit in perpetual sadness, immobilized by the gravity of my loss, or I can choose to rise from the pain and treasure the most precious gift I have, life itself."[1]

I understood from the beginning the importance of sitting in sadness, of being immobilized by the gravity of my loss. What I couldn't comprehend was how to rise from the pain and treasure my life again.

My story is intertwined with my faith in God, his Son Jesus Christ, and in their words. I personally use the King James Version of the Bible, and I'll share its verses with you. If your faith or spiritual practices look different than mine when I share my story, please reflect on your own spirituality and how it has influenced your life.

Throughout all my trials, God has supported me before, during, and after in his most glorious ways. During the most painful days, I couldn't always feel his support even when it was there, but I could remember. I could remember the times in the past when I had felt his support and I clung to those memories.

Repeatedly, and in different ways, God has whispered to me, *I helped you before, I'll help you again*, reminding me to trust in his goodwill and love.

As I share my story, my overarching desire is for you to feel and hear that there is always hope. Always.

Disclaimer: I share my experiences from my point of view and as truthfully as possible, but I recognize that it may be different from someone else's memories of the same event. Also, some of the names have been changed to protect their identity.

NOTE

1. Walter Anderson, *Meant to Be* (New York: Harper Perennial, 2004). See goodreads.com/author/quotes/278436.Walter_Anderson. Accessed June 2, 2020.

CHAPTER 1

Mother's Day

I found my fortress, in You
And my soul is anchored, with You
My resting place, is in Your name
Forever safe[1]

—Lee Brown

My birthday landed on the day before Mother's Day in 2007. I decided we would celebrate in a couple of weeks when I returned from a planned trip. Every day with our six children was filled with activity, and there was no time for a celebration that busy Saturday.

Our oldest daughter, twenty-year-old Stephanie, was away from home, a college sophomore in Idaho, but everyone else's activities kept us hopping all day.

Our ten-year-old daughter, Carrie, spent the day performing in a homeschool Shakespeare play with her older brothers while I attended a mandatory Cub Scout leader meeting for an upcoming day camp for eight-year-old David.

I went to my meeting reluctantly, resenting having to miss the final play performance. I had seen it earlier in the week, and I was grateful for that.

That same Saturday, our eighteen-year-old daughter, Kristin, frantically prepared to go to her senior prom that night. She had designed and sewn her own dress, but the fabric turned out to be faulty and was literally coming apart at the seams.

No dress, no prom. Preparing for the prom became an unexpectedly huge ordeal. In between other demands, I hurriedly helped Kristin with a solution to the dress fiasco. We made frantic phone calls to friends in hopes of finding an alternative gown for her to wear. Just in time, she found something suitable.

Kristin made temporary repairs to the dress she had created and chose to wear that for pictures, but knowing it wouldn't hold up on the dance floor, she brought the borrowed dress to change into as soon as pictures were over. She dressed and finished her preparations moments before her boyfriend, Joel, picked her up for the evening. I followed Kristin and Joel to their friend's house to take pictures of them and their prom group before they all left for dinner.

While Kristin was at the prom, my husband Ron and I attended a parent appreciation dinner hosted by the teens of our homeschool group. Carrie was only ten and officially not a teen, but she was invited to attend with her older brothers, James (twelve) and Dallin (fifteen). She was thrilled!

Carrie served us all night long. She was constantly asking if we needed something else. She brought us water. She brought us rolls. She loved feeling so grown up and included, and it was her nature to be so service minded and loving. She was in her element.

Still too young and immature for the dinner event, our eight-year-old son, David, spent the evening with a friend who lived in the neighborhood just a few streets away. Even though his friend lived close by, it was the first time David had been allowed to ride his bike to his friend's house on his own.

Energetic David was very adventurous, so it was all we could do to keep him contained and safe, but the day had finally come for a little more freedom. David had looked forward to this day when he could explore further from home.

After a long and demanding day, Ron kept the kids up watching the movie *Facing the Giants*, while I quickly packed so I could go to bed as early as possible. I wanted plenty of rest before our long road trip.

Early the next morning, James, Carrie, David, and I planned to drive from our home just north of Houston to Ron's parents' home in Murphy, North Carolina, on the western tip of the state, a couple of hours north of Atlanta, Georgia. With our large family and our extended families so far away, we were used to piling in the car and driving across country. We had made this trek many times before.

I went to bed irritated that Ron was keeping the little kids up late. I wanted them to get their sleep, so I wouldn't have to deal with tired, grumpy kids the next day, but they stayed up and I went to bed.

David snuggled up on one side of his dad and Carrie on the other as they watched the movie. I know now that this was just how it was meant to be, and I regret my irritation. They were meant to have that very special time with their dad before they were gone.

At 5:00 a.m. the next morning, Mother's Day, we gathered on the long driveway of our Spring, Texas, home. Ron helped me pack our luggage into the back of our GMC Yukon, an SUV that was a necessity for our family. Ron had a knack for making everything fit. After he worked his magic, we were loaded to go.

Our three youngest children and I were squeezing in a visit to their grandparents' country home. They lived on five acres in the hills of southwest North Carolina, and the land was a kid's paradise. Lots of room to roam among the trees, a fire pit behind the house for roasting hotdogs and marshmallows, a creek beyond the fire pit at the bottom of the property, and tractor rides provided by their grandpa. It's as close as you can get to camping and still sleep in a warm bed.

Our son James loaded up his heavy backpack into the front seat. He carried that heavy backpack full of books and other treasures everywhere he went. I'm not sure he ever read any of the books in his bag, but he always had it with him.

Carrie and David climbed into the backseat with a couple dozen toys and activities to keep them busy on the long day's drive. I threw in cheese crackers, raisins, and other snacks in an effort to keep them happy so I could focus on my job, which was driving.

Ron gave us each a hug and a kiss. As he hugged me goodbye, he added his usual reminder, "Be safe, and remember you have precious cargo."

As we drove, Carrie and David happily played together in the back seat, entertaining themselves with their toys as we traveled through East Texas, Louisiana, and into Mississippi.

As we entered Mississippi on Interstate 10, I had to admit the trip was going great. I was surprised and thrilled that the grumpy outbursts from tired kids had not materialized.

In the early afternoon, we stopped for lunch at Taco Bell. I was feeling generous because of their good behavior, and I encouraged the kids to order whatever they wanted from the menu, an unexpected treat from a thrifty mom who was typically worried about getting every penny out of every dollar.

After our lunch break, we jumped back into the Yukon to continue our journey east. Traveling on interstate 20, I teased James, who was sitting next to me in the front seat. I pulled the SUV slowly to the right and ran over the rumble strips on the side of the highway. We giggled at the funny noises the tires made against the uneven pavement.

As we drove, we listened to music. It was Sunday, and we normally would have been at church, so I brought some inspirational music to enjoy. I particularly remember listening to the CD *Joseph* by the Nashville Tribute Band, music dedicated to the life and mission of Joseph Smith Jr., a church leader.

The song that caught my interest was "Emma," a song dedicated to Emma Smith, Joseph's wife. I could feel Emma's pain as I listened to the haunting verse that foreshadowed my own pain. "When you buried your children, I'm sure the angels stood in reverence as you prayed. How much can one heart take, how much can one heart take?" I reflected on the unimaginable pain of losing a child.

Eventually, the peace in the backseat deteriorated. Carrie got frustrated with David pestering her.

I looked behind me to remind David for at least the third time to put his seat belt back on. These were the days before it was well known that car seats were safer beyond preschool, so everyone was just strapped into their individual seat belts.

As I looked back over my right shoulder, I watched Carrie slide from the middle seat next to David to the seat behind me next to the door. As she latched her seat belt, she said, "I love you, Mom. Happy Mother's Day."

Everyone settled in for the last of our drive, and I thought I would make it before dark.

Sometime later, as we neared the Mississippi, Alabama, border, I woke up to our SUV bumping along in the grassy median between the eastbound lanes and the westbound lanes of highway. I had never even felt sleepy!

In shock, I tried to bring the SUV back up onto the road. When I did, our vehicle started to roll.

It rolled and rolled, and rolled, and rolled—impossible to count how many times. I remember hearing a voice as we rolled. "Bring your arm in," the voice urged. Somehow, I had the sense to obey, and I pulled my left arm closer to my body.

We rolled across the eastbound highway until we finally came to a stop, upright on our wheels, facing the highway on the grassy right shoulder of the eastbound lane.

When we landed, I couldn't see anything. It was midday, but everything was dark. I had temporarily lost my sight when I hit my head as we tumbled.

Even though I couldn't see anything, I instinctively and immediately knew that our lives had changed forever. I heard James crying in distress beside me. His cries frightened me since I couldn't determine how injured he was. At the same time, I was grateful for those cries, because at least I knew he was alive.

I frantically called out for Carrie and David, but there was no response. "Carrie! David! Carrie! David! Are you all right? Carrie! David!" Silence.

Slowly, my eyesight started to return. I sat in the front seat, physically stunned and paralyzed with fear. As I looked at the devastation of our vehicle—the shattered glass, the mangled mess of the vehicle, our strewn belongings, and the terrible silence from the back seat—I screamed in agony, "I killed my kids! I killed my kids! I killed my kids!"

The memory of those anguished screams haunt me today as I reflect on my suffering twelve-year-old son crying next to me and witnessing such a horrifying scene.

I couldn't find my cell phone, but I was desperate to call Ron. I noticed people gathering in the field, yards away from where we came to a stop. The realization punched me hard that Carrie and David were in the grass, thrown from the vehicle during the violent rolling.

A man approached the car. "I need a phone! I need to call my husband!" I cried. He handed me his cell phone, and I dialed Ron with panic and dread.

"Ron, I've been in an accident and Carrie and David have been thrown from the car," I blurted out between sobs. My voice dropped as I continued, "I don't know if they're going to make it."

I could feel his anguish across the connection. I could sense his shock with his stunned response. "Okay, it will be okay. It will be okay," he said to soothe me, but I could hear the fear in his voice. "Where are you?" he asked.

I had a sense that Carrie and David were either both going to survive, or they were going to die together. As siblings, they had an unusually close bond, and I couldn't imagine one without the other.

The sweet man who loaned me his phone stayed with me, talking slowly and softly, trying to keep me calm. He said that his wife and others were with Carrie and David, that they were okay, and that his wife was singing to Carrie to comfort her. I could see people in the distance standing over my children, using blankets to shield them from the intense afternoon sun.

When I look back on this scene, I remember so many people in that field with Carrie and David, but I don't remember many cars parked on the side of the highway. I wonder if I was witnessing heavenly angels as well as earthly angels in that grass along the interstate. Regardless of what I saw, I have no doubt that many angels were present.

Emergency vehicles started to arrive. Carrie and David seemed miles away, and I could barely make out the scene as the paramedics loaded David onto a stretcher, his small arm slipping from under the sheet and dangling off the side as they carried him to the ambulance.

Another paramedic crew cautiously took James and then me out of the car and placed us on Stryker boards to keep us stabilized while we were transported to the hospital.

James and I were taken to Rush Hospital in Meridian, Mississippi. Someone—I don't remember who—told me that Carrie and David were rushed to a hospital in York, Alabama. We were that close to the state border.

I didn't understand why they were taken to a different hospital, but I didn't ask. To this day, I assume it is because they were both small country hospitals ill-equipped for multiple emergency cases on a holiday afternoon, but I'm not sure.

In the ambulance, I asked repeatedly if Carrie and David were okay, but no one responded.

Once at the hospital and in tremendous physical and emotional pain, I laid on the Stryker board vacillating between quiet tears and an unearthly peace as I imagined the Savior there carrying my burdens.

A few weeks before the accident, a friend had walked me through a Christ-centered visualization. She guided me through while asking questions. "If you were to imagine a peaceful place where you could meet the Savior, where would it be?" she asked.

I described a spring meadow filled with foot-high grass and colorful wildflowers surrounded on all sides in the distance by Rocky Mountains with delicate snowcaps. I could see, smell, and hear the meadow as if I were there, even though my experiences had mostly been along the white sandy beaches of Florida where I grew up.

As I stood in the meadow, Jesus Christ approached me, accepted my burdens, and offered me indescribable love and compassion. In return, I offered him a boxed gift. When my friend asked what was in the box, I said, "music"—a very unequal exchange.

As Luke reminds us in Luke 17:10, "When ye shall have done all those things which are commanded you, say, we are unprofitable servants." What the Lord offers us will always outweigh what we have to offer him.

I had never experienced a meditative visualization like that before, and the power of the experience surprised me. Little did I know that I would so desperately need the peace of that vision just a few short weeks later.

James was being attended to in another room nearby. Still, no one would tell me anything about Carrie and David's condition. An emergency room nurse did tell me that my aunt Ava and her husband David, who lived in Richton, Mississippi, just an hour and a half from Meridian, were on their way to the hospital. I gratefully anticipated friendly family faces.

In the meantime, I had a visit from a highway patrolman asking questions about where we were traveling from and to, who was in the car, what happened, etc. I answered as best I could in my distracted and pained state.

Someone had contacted a local bishop (the congregation leaders of our church) to visit me in the hospital until my family could arrive. He sat by my cot, clearly uncomfortable, as he tried to say something to reassure a stranger.

He talked about the eternal nature of life and that regardless of what happened to Carrie and David, they would always be mine. I knew all that, but I didn't have the strength to respond. The pain was too great, and it was far too soon to talk about eternal life. I can't imagine the courage it took for him to show up at the hospital.

My Aunt Ava and Uncle David finally arrived. Ron was at the Houston airport trying to get a flight to Mississippi as quickly as possible, and my aunt put him on the phone to talk to me. I hadn't talked to Ron since the first phone call.

"Julie," Ron paused. "Carrie and David didn't make it," he whispered. The conversation ended. We were both crying, and we hung up knowing that life would never be the same.

––––––––

NOTE

1. Lee Brown, "Safe." See genius.com/Victory-worship-safe-lyrics. Accessed June 2, 2020.

Carrie and David, Idaho Falls, 2005

CHAPTER 2

The Long Journey Home

As surely as there is a voyage away, there is a journey home.[1]

—Jack Kornfield

Just after I received the horrific news of Carrie's and David's deaths, I learned that James was being prepared for emergency surgery. His right leg, which was next to the door of the car, had sustained the brunt of the impact during the accident and was severely broken.

After CT Scans to insure it was safe, the hospital attendants took me off the Stryker board and moved me to a temporary cot. They wheeled me in on the cot to where James laid frightened and nervous. I held his hand and tried to reassure him that he would be all right. We didn't talk about Carrie and David. It wasn't the time to share that news with him.

After a long, tragic day, Ron finally arrived at the hospital. James's surgery went well, but he was in a lot of pain. The surgical procedure involved long incisions down the front and the back of his right calf to relieve pressure from the swelling.

The hospital and staff were amazing. One of the residents shared his shock that Dr. Sonny Rush was there at the hospital on Mother's Day to perform James's surgery. The hospital was named after Dr. Rush's family, and the procedure he performed for James was one that he had pioneered. This was one of the many miracles within the tragedy.

My injuries weren't as serious. I had a broken wrist, sprained shoulders, a concussion, and a lot of bruising, including dark bruising around my eyes from the force of the accident.

They admitted James and me and assigned us the same hospital room. Outside of our room was a large, private sitting area, where our family and friends started to gather.

My sister, Kari, and my mother, Nancy, came from Nashville; my brother, James, from Michigan; my Aunt Ava and Uncle David from Mississippi; my Aunt Kathy from Salt Lake City; my dad, Jim, from Florida; and two of Ron's closest friends, Paul and Jason, from Houston, all gathered in support.

The extra space they gave us at the hospital was a tremendous blessing. Our family and friends held vigil in the hospital with us for days—a symbol of their love and strength.

After I was settled into the hospital room that night, my dear friend Rachel called me from Texas to express her sorrow and sadness. She loved Carrie and David too. Her daughter Sarah and her son Davis were some of their closest friends.

When Rachel called, I told her, "Carrie and David are forever safe." They would no longer have to struggle with the hardships of this mortal life. It felt like an odd thing to say, but I truly did believe that they were safely in their Savior's arms, as unbearable as that reality was for me.

As a young married mom of two small boys almost two years old and seven weeks old, Rachel lost her first husband in a plane crash that not only left her a widow at twenty-one years old, but also claimed the life of her father-in-law. Having traveled through tremendous pain, she was prepared to show up, and she played a significant role of support in the months to come.

I marvel at our family and friends' strength to be with us in those shocking, sorrowful days. Before the accident, I was frequently unwilling to show up for the tough stuff. I felt awkward and unprepared to say the right things.

Remembering my own inadequacy, I decided while I was still in the hospital that I would not be offended by anything anyone said. I determined that this was hard for everyone, and anything anyone said was meant to help, not harm, and I would look at it that way. It was pure inspiration that served me well and saved me from additional suffering.

The day after the accident, Ron had to go to the morgue to identify Carrie and David's bodies. His friends Jason and Paul accompanied him and offered needed support for this awful task. I don't know how he did it, but he told me later it was as if they were lying there asleep. To him they looked peaceful, and he said he felt their presence with him, comforting him.

He also had to deal with the police report, gathering our things from the Yukon, and trying to recover some of our belongings that had been scattered down the highway. Dealing with all the logistics became his arduous task for several months.

The next night after the accident, James awoke to a darkened room. He was coherent enough to quietly ask his dad about Carrie and David. I listened from the adjacent bed as Ron gently shared the devastating news. "They didn't make it, James." James and his dad collapsed together in mournful sobs.

After several days in the hospital, James was recovering but still had healing hurdles ahead of him. He needed to heal, we needed to get back to Spring to plan a funeral, and there was a dispute among the attending doctors.

The general attending physician did not want to release James. He was concerned about him traveling the many miles back to Texas in his condition, and James still needed another surgical procedure in a week or two to finish the work of the first surgery.

Fortunately, James's surgeon, Dr. Rush, a kind and gentle man, understood the importance of us getting back for a funeral. He gave his consent to release James and made arrangements to work with a doctor in Texas to continue James's care.

The night before James's release, I was released from the hospital. I don't know why they kept me in the hospital so long. It wasn't physically necessary, but I felt safer in the hospital than anywhere else at that point.

I went back to a hotel room with my mom, my sister, and my aunts. It didn't feel right to be walking around. I felt completely strange and numb. I didn't know how to act or what to say. Nothing felt natural or normal.

The next morning the nurses and attendants showered James with all the love they had been sharing with him all week. They lined the hallway, cried, and waved as we walked past them to the elevator in a slow, sad procession. Ron and I followed behind James's wheelchair with a cart of flowers and gifts from friends.

Ron and my sister, Kari, had figured out a way to place James in the back of her van with his heavily splinted leg propped up, with lots of pillows and blankets between him and the second row of seats. His leg was not healed enough to be in a cast, so they had splinted and wrapped it in layers of bandages and cushioning materials. Despite their planning, it was difficult maneuvering James into the backseat. With him finally in position, we started the long trip home, back the way we had come.

I know it was painful for James, but he hardly complained the whole trip. Fortunately, he was still on strong painkillers. Even though my injuries were not severe, the drive home was excruciating as we made our way back on the highways I had traveled the week before, never reaching my destination.

I sat behind my sister who was driving. Kari's a great driver, but I felt like I was in danger the entire trip. I didn't know what to call it then, but I do now. I was experiencing Post-Traumatic Stress Disorder (PTSD) from the rollover accident. Every bump, every turn, every use of the brake, sent me into high alert.

Our three older children, Stephanie, who had flown home from college, Kristin, a senior in high school, and our fifteen-year-old son, Dallin, were all waiting for us to get home. I learned from my friends later that Stephanie had been amazing, taking charge while we were away and organizing the many volunteers that came to the house to prepare for our return.

We were happy to be reunited with Stephanie, Dallin, and Kristin, but our arrival was a solemn occasion with lots of tears and hugs. A twin bed had been set up for James in the living room of our home since he was unable to climb the stairs to his second-floor bedroom.

Thanks to many volunteers from our church and neighborhood, the house was spotless, with bowls of fruit in the kitchen, a stocked refrigerator, and fresh flowers and gifts on the counters. Even our yard had received love, with newly planted flowers in the flower beds, lovingly planted by the families of our homeschool group.

Our home felt painfully sad but sacred.

NOTE

1. Jack Kornfield, *After the Ecstasy, the Laundry* (New York: Bantam, 2001).

CLUFF

OUR BELOVED SON
DAVID BENJAMIN
SEPT. 29. 1998
MAY 13. 2007

OUR LOVING DAUGHTER
CARRIE ELIZABETH
SEPT. 20. 1996
MAY 13. 2007

CHILD OF GOD

CHAPTER 3

Burying Our Children

Pain insists upon being attended to. God whispers to us in our pleasures, speaks in our consciences, but shouts in our pains. It is his megaphone to rouse a deaf world.[1]

—C. S. Lewis

Oddly, I don't remember anything about the devastating phone call late one night in March 1990. But I do remember my reaction after receiving the news.

I stood beside my washing machine, screaming and crying to my brother who was in a hospital bed hundreds of miles away, fighting for his life after a self-inflicted gunshot wound to his head. The prognosis was dismal. "How could you do this? How is this possible? Why? Why? Why? Why? Why?"

In a distraught trance, I continued to move the damp laundry from the machine to the dryer while my heart broke into a million pieces. My mind searched for a way for this reality to be fiction. If I rejected this truth, could I change the outcome? The answer was no, and within a few hours, John was removed from life support.

Everything between my screaming tantrum and getting on a flight from my home in Palm Harbor, Florida, to Salt Lake City, Utah, for John's funeral is forgotten, but I must have folded and put away the laundry, arranged for my three-year-old and eighteen-month-old daughters to be cared for by friends, ordered plane tickets, and arrived at the airport on time for the first leg of a miserable trip.

I landed in Utah in time for an open casket viewing, but I struggled to look at John and his makeup-covered wound, evidence of the harm that was inflicted on him and took his life. Disconnected from everything that was happening around me, I numbly stepped into the hallway. From around the corner, I overheard my mother say to someone, "I'm worried about Julie. She's not crying."

You didn't see my screaming and crying before I got here, I thought.

Like scenes in a movie, my mind recalls specific moments that fade in and out of memory. The next scene was a funeral service at the funeral home.

My sister-in-law's sister played the piano as we agonizingly sang songs of worship and hope, knowing that we were burying a son, a brother, a husband, and a friend. In our dazed state, no one had remembered to arrange for someone to lead the music, so we glanced around for a second and then began to sing without a chorister.

My uncle gave a beautiful eulogy, remembering John's athletic ability on the baseball field, his intelligence, and his likable and amusing personality. The local bishop shared his message of hope in Christ, but not knowing our family, he mispronounced John's wife's name and stumbled over a few other details.

The messages of hope floated over our heads and dissipated out the window. One day we would be able to allow the messages to enter our hearts, but not right then. Not when the pain was ever present and consuming.

After gathering with family and friends for the service in Utah, we traveled back to Florida for John's burial. I accompanied my parents to visit the funeral home and make the final arrangements for John's burial site, headstone, and graveside services.

I felt indescribable emptiness as we walked through all the logistics that had to be handled. It was as if I was in a costume and was peering out an unclear mask that obstructed my ability to interact with my world.

I wasn't present. I wasn't anywhere. I simply existed because my heart still beat. My lungs still took in air, but everything else was beyond my capacity. Somehow in their extreme shock and sadness, my mother and father were able to take care of what had to be done.

A few days later, the hearse picked us up at my mother and father's home and drove us to the cemetery where, surrounded by our family and friends, we once again remembered John's life and our intense sorrow at losing him at only twenty-three years old.

After the dedicatory prayer over his grave, I stood in the spring air, hiding behind dark sunglasses and accepting hugs and condolences from our friends before we started the silent trip back to the house.

Church friends had prepared a lunch for us at my parent's home. The food was abundant even though my appetite wasn't, but I spooned up an obligatory plate and sat in the family room as my family, plates in hand, gathered in a solemn circle. This awkward gathering slowly opened to casual conversation that eventually lead to a joke or two and a spattering of nervous laughter.

How could I be laughing? Was it okay to laugh? How dare I laugh when my wonderful, beautiful, funny brother was dead.

If John was here, if we weren't in so much pain, we would all be laughing. And John would be leading the way with his quick wit and comedic prowess, standing in front of us with a stand-up routine that would rival any TV comedy special. In fact, there are glimpses of John's impromptu routines in the background of my wedding reception video just five years before as he performed Johnny Carson impersonations with his twin brother, James.

But for now, everything had changed, and laughing was no longer acceptable. Joy was no longer an option. Hope for the future was a distant shadow in the past.

John's death was my first introduction to the devastation of loss and the bleak realities of grief. Of course, I had experienced other losses and other disappointments, but none before this had thrust me into grief the way that losing my brother did.

A couple of months later, I played in my first casual tennis tournament. I debated whether to play, because I wasn't sure I wanted to show up in a social situation and attempt to compete.

Eventually I decided to go. As I played, I forgot about my brother and my pain for a few minutes. When I realized that I had been distracted from remembering John, I felt a mix of relief for the reprieve and guilt for my disloyalty.

Over time, John's death wasn't so predominant in my day-to-day living, and I learned to adapt to the reality that he had moved on into the next life before us. I even learned to feel the joy and hope of life again. This was the beginning of my experience with loss, grief, and healing, but it certainly wasn't the end.

As we prepared for Carrie and David's funeral, I reflected on my brother's death seventeen years before. Once again, I felt the strange emptiness of tragedy and loss. Once again, I felt like the stranger behind the mask, unable to see her world clearly. But that tragic loss of my brother prepared me to bury my children.

Not only was I more familiar with funeral homes, burials, and funeral services, I was also familiar with loss, grief, and eventual healing. I remembered that I healed from my grief of losing John even though I will always remember and love my brother. The healing I had experienced before gave me the tiniest glimmer of hope that I could heal again. The trauma of losing my children was different than losing my brother, but at least I had some knowledge of the grief experience.

Ron and I visited the funeral home right away after traveling home from Mississippi. Making the final arrangements for Carrie's and David's bodies was a necessary task, and no matter how dreadful, we wanted to honor them with these last acts of care for their bodies.

We sat across from the funeral director with solemn attention.

I wore dark sunglasses even indoors to hide my black eyes from the impact of the accident. Ron assured me it wasn't necessary, but I felt compelled to hide behind the glasses. The funeral director shared his condolences with us and explained that they were not in the business to make money on burying children.

As a practice, and as much as possible, they offered their services for free in these dreadful circumstances, including a burial plot and basic caskets. We gratefully agreed to that arrangement. While we lived comfortably, the financial strain of an unexpected funeral was an added burden to the already unthinkable load we were carrying.

We continued to discuss all the unpleasantries, including where Carrie and David would be buried and how they would be buried. Their last resting place would be in a large, wooded cemetery in Tomball, Texas, just a few miles north of our house. A grave would be dug on one plot that would allow them to bury their caskets one on top of the other. Not only was this sensible, it seemed fitting for Carrie and David to be buried together and share a burial plaque.

Day after day, Ron continued to bear the weight of the funeral arrangements, the household, James's and my healing, and coordinating with everyone who wanted to help. With some assistance from our families, he prepared a proper obituary that would in a few short lines honor their beautiful lives.

CARRIE ELIZABETH CLUFF and DAVID BENJAMIN CLUFF returned to their Heavenly Father on Mother's Day, Sunday, May 13th, 2007.

Carrie was born on September 20, 1996, and David was born on September 29, 1998, to Ronald Verl Cluff Jr. and Julie Wells Cluff. Both beloved children were born in Lewisville, Texas.

They are survived by their parents, Ron and Julie Cluff; sisters, Stephanie and Kristin; brothers, Dallin and James; paternal grandparents, Ronald Verl Cluff Sr. and Elizabeth Anne Cluff; and their maternal grandparents, James Raymond Wells and Nancy DeLoach Wells.

Carrie was known by all who knew and loved her as Sweet Carrie or Care Bear. Forever on her lips was a ready smile and a song. She liked to give hugs to show her love.

David can only be described as a moving, fun loving, creative, and bright child. His smile would warm every heart for miles and gave joy to everyone.

Though their time on earth was short, their lives were well lived as happy, peacemaking, and loving children. They will be greatly missed. Their father will forever cherish the daily arrival home with both children running toward the car screaming, "Daddy's home, Daddy's home!!"

"In life they were not divided and in death they were not separated."[2]

—John Taylor

As the funeral approached, Ron was adamant about speaking at the service. During our discussions, I was often lying in bed, recovering, and Ron sat in the upholstered rocking chair next to me. As I listened to his thoughts from my prone position, I could not imagine speaking at the funeral, and I discouraged him from attempting it. "It would be too hard," I told him.

He explained his need to share with our friends and family that we would be okay because we understood God's plan of salvation. We knew Carrie and David were in our Heavenly Father's hands, that they were okay, and that we would eventually be reunited with them in heaven. Because we knew that, even though life would be painful and hard during this separation, we would survive. We would be able to navigate this terrible experience knowing that Carrie and David were safely in God's home.

Despite how difficult this time was, Ron and I both felt the strengthening power of God's love for us. I believe this is the "earnest of the spirit," God's confirmation of our faith. Paul explains in 2 Corinthians that God provides "earnest of the Spirit in our hearts" (2:22).

When we put earnest money down to bind a contract, we are saying that we intend to pay the full amount of the contract. The earnest money is the promise of our intent to follow through. In this same way, the whisperings of the Spirit that we experience is an earnest of the promised blessings God has made with his children.

The Spirit of God we felt in preparation for the funeral service and during the service was the "earnest of the Spirit in our hearts" that we would eventually be reunited with Carrie and David in heaven in the eternities.

We continued to prepare for the service with the help of our family and friends. Jason, our friend who had flown to Mississippi after the accident and the father of three of Carrie and David's closest friends, agreed to share their life sketch. Another friend and church leader, Mike, agreed to talk about David, and one of Carrie's church teachers, Ann, consented to speak as well. Ron and our bishop rounded out the speakers.

The week before the accident, Ron, Carrie, David, and I attended the high school pop concert to hear our daughter Kristin sing. She was always shy about her singing, and I could never persuade her to practice for us, so I wasn't certain what she had planned.

As she sang "Somebody's Hero," I cried silent tears as I reflected on the tender moments I had shared with Kristin through the years and how in less than a month she would graduate from high school, leave for college, and move into adulthood, with her own home, her own struggles, and her own ambitions.

Kristin sweetly sang the words of appreciation of a daughter to a mother who had sacrificed so much to be her hero.[3] My heart burst with pride in my beautiful daughter and hoped that I had been her hero too. Days later after the accident, the memories of this song that Kristin chose rang in my mind as I hoped beyond any possible hope that I was still a good mother despite the horrific accident.

During the concert, we sat next to our friends whose son was also performing that night. Carrie was happy to have their daughter and her friend's company during the performance. As the song "You Lift Me Up" was performed, I learned later that Carrie leaned over to her friend and told her it was her favorite song.

Now a couple of weeks later, we were planning a funeral, and I was eager to have inspiring music at the service. My sister suggested that her son Chase could play a piano solo he had been practicing, and the song he had prepared was "You Lift Me Up."

"Yes, please," I quickly replied. Chase is Carrie's cousin, born only twelve days after her. They had been inseparable whenever we were together. Chase was a great pianist even at ten years old, and having him honor the kids with that piece for the funeral was wonderful.

After the funeral, my friend JoLynn shared with me what Carrie said to her daughter about that song being her favorite at the concert a few weeks before. It's no accident that Chase had prepared that song, which became a tender gift from heaven to my heart.

JoLynn offered that her son Taylor had been practicing a new song also, which he was willing to sing at the service. Taylor was one of Kristin's friends and has an exceptional tenor voice. Even as a senior in high school, his talent was indisputable.

He ended the funeral with an exquisite rendition of "Oh Lord, My Redeemer."[4] Through the power of music, Taylor lifted us with remembrances of Jesus's love and sacrifice as he sang, "Oh Lord, my Redeemer, Thou has done so much for me! Oh Lord, my Redeemer, All my love I give to Thee!" The outpouring of the Spirit was profound.

Finally, our daughters Kristin and Stephanie expressed their desire to sing a duet. They had an arrangement of the hymn "Abide with Me, 'Tis Eventide." Their sweet voices and tender feelings rang through the chapel as they shared, "O Savior, stay this night with me; Behold, 'tis eventide."

> Abide with me; 'tis eventide,
> And lone will be the night
> If I cannot commune with thee
> Nor find in thee my light.
> The darkness of the world, I fear,
> Would in my home abide.
>
> O Savior, stay this night with me;
> Behold, 'tis eventide.[5]

The morning of the service, we arrived early with our family for the public viewing. I wore a long white tunic with subtle black stripes and a long black skirt, sunglasses to hide my bruised eyes, and a sling to protect my broken wrist.

The funeral home had rolled Carrie's and David's caskets into a large classroom in the church for the viewing before the service. Carrie was in an open pink casket and David was in an open blue one. The funeral home had decided to upgrade their caskets to these colorful choices as a gesture of support and compassion.

I didn't recognize either of our children. My friend, Jennifer, Jason's wife, had helped me pick out and shop for clothing for Carrie and David to be buried in, and without the familiar clothing and my knowledge of why we were there, I wouldn't have known it was them.

Carrie's face was bloated, and her beautiful curls were arranged in a frizzy array around the pillow. David looked like a plastic doll. Without his lively personality, he didn't look real.

I remembered Ron's description after he saw them the morning after the car crash when he went to the morgue to identify their bodies. He relayed that they had looked peaceful and like they were sleeping. I longed to see them like that. But despite their appearance, I stood over their lifeless bodies, touching their hands to say my goodbyes.

A long line of people streamed through the room to offer personal condolences. I'm not sure what I said. The usual "thank you"? "I don't know how we'll do it either"? "Yes, it's shocking and hard, but we'll be okay"? I'm not sure.

But I felt responsible to do and say the right thing to make people comfortable in an extremely uncomfortable situation. Why do we do that? Why can't we all just agree that it's uncomfortable and be okay with the discomfort? No phrase that anyone offered me or that I offered them was going to make things right or even slightly better in that moment.

Guests left the room as we shut the door and gathered with our family to close the caskets and offer a prayer before we joined the more than nine hundred people gathered in the chapel of the church.

All eyes solemnly looked on as two caskets, pink and blue, were rolled into the chapel followed by our family, including grandparents, aunts, uncles, cousins, siblings, and spouses. We filed into our seats in the reserved pews up front to witness a funeral service for two beautiful children who left this life sooner than anyone could have predicted.

It was May 21. Only eight days since the accident, and James was in no condition to attend the funeral. Under normal circumstances, he would have been recuperating at home with no plans of leaving the house for at least another couple of weeks. But the circumstances were far from normal, so instead, we rented a wheelchair so he could attend the service. With his leg propped up, he sat in the aisle next to the bench where we sat. He soon fell asleep from exhaustion and painkillers.

Despite my efforts to talk him out of it, Ron offered a wonderful memorial and testimony. I don't know how he did it, but I'm grateful he did. He expressed his love for Carrie and David, his gratitude that James and I were still here, and his testimony of the promises of the resurrection and life beyond this existence through the power of Jesus Christ.

When the last words were spoken and the last notes were sung, we left the chapel to take our children to the cemetery for their burial.

For several months, Ron and I deliberated over the tombstone that would mark their grave. Eventually, we found a painting of Jesus sitting with two children at his knees—a boy on his right, and a girl on his left.

We took the picture to the funeral home and asked if they could sketch this into the stone, which they did on the upper right. Their stone reads, "Our Beloved Son David Benjamin, Sept. 29, 1998–May 13, 2007" and "Our Loving Daughter Carrie Elizabeth, Sept. 20, 1996–May 13, 2007," with their surname at the top of the stone and music notes and the first line of a favorite song, "I am a child of God" at the bottom.

———

NOTES

1. C. S. Lewis, *The Problem of Pain*, revised edition (New York: Harper One, 2015).

2. Doctrine and Covenants 135:3.

3. Jamie O'Neal, Ed Hill, and Shaye Smith, "Somebody's Hero" (Nashville: Capitol, 2005). See youtube.com/watch?v=1_uMQTw7v2g.

4. Jeff Goodrich, "Oh Lord, My Redeemer," from the songbook *I Heard Him Come* (Salt Lake City: Deseret Book, 1990).

5. Lowrie M. Hofford (words) and Harrison Millard (music), "Abide with Me; 'Tis Eventide," *Hymns*, no. 165 (Salt Lake City: The Church of Jesus Christ of Latter-day Saints, 1985).

CHAPTER 4

Remembering

Fear thou not; for I am with thee: be not dismayed; for I
am thy God: I will strengthen thee; yea, I will help thee; yea,
I will uphold thee with the right hand of my righteousness.

—Isaiah 41:10

Soon our families and friends returned home to their families and their lives in Florida, Michigan, Mississippi, Utah, Tennessee, and other areas across the country. As the protection of shock wore off, we were left with our stark reality.

The gloom encompassed our home like damp, dark prison walls that don't allow comfort or escape. My mind was a torture chamber of re-crimination, blame, and bitter accusations. I had nowhere to run from my continuous and brutal torment. My days became lonely, dark, and hopeless.

I was attracted to music and TV shows that matched the state of my mind—hollow and dreary. With little motivation to do anything else, I turned to mindless, hopeless entertainment to distract me from my suffering, which was equally sorrow over the loss of my children and regret for the manner in which they died. My mind was consumed with grief.

Despite my sadness, I had learned from past experiences to lean on God. I knew that he knew me, and he loved me, but I still didn't know how he could allow such an event to occur. I had spent years learning to hear God, to hear the quiet whisperings of the Holy Spirit, to listen and understand through spiritual eyes, and I was determined to gain an understanding of what happened and why.

In between mindless entertainment, long jags of desperate tears, and endless torment, I searched for meaning. I read everything I could find on near-death experiences, the meaning of death, the state of heaven, and how to overcome trials and adversity. I cried out in agony for a snippet of peace and comfort.

Because I was so consumed with grief, I discovered it was difficult to feel inspired or to feel God's presence in my life like I had before. My emotions were overwhelmed, and in that overwhelmed state, my spiritual sensitivities were overwhelmed as well.

Because I could not feel the strength of my faith, it would have been easy to deny my beliefs, blame God, and walk away from him in anger and bitterness because of what he allowed to happen. I felt the pull of the daily struggle between turning to a God I had always depended on but could no longer feel, and running away from him in white-hot anger and distress. And then I would remember Peter's answer to Jesus: "Lord, to whom shall we go? Thou hast the words of eternal life. And we believe and are sure that thou art that Christ, the Son of the Living God" (John 6:68–69).

My choice was clear. I could stay with my convictions and work through my devastating pain and anguish with God's help, or I could run from the only true peace and solace available to me.

I decided to stay. I decided to lean on God. I decided that no matter how long it took, I was going to regain my spiritual footing somehow, some way. It was the only option.

I began to depend on past experiences when I had felt the whisperings of the Spirit and exercised faith and hope; those times when my faith had been answered in remarkable and undeniable ways. I chose to remember, and those "rememberings" became my anchor during my darkest days, each experience a miracle in the darkness.

As a single mom of three young children after my divorce from my first husband and just a couple of years after my brother died, I was suddenly thrust into the position of providing financially for my little family. I needed to buy food, pay the mortgage, pay all the bills including the utilities, and make a car payment. Everything. And God provided for our every need.

Before I formally separated from my husband, a friend called and asked if I would be willing to do some work for his company. Craig knew I had a background in insurance, and as the COO of a growing, small, durable medical equipment company, he needed someone to prepare forms for claim submissions to health insurance companies.

He thought I might be looking for something since I had previously been working for my husband's insurance office, which had closed a few weeks before. I agreed to help, and I started shortly thereafter.

My main responsibilities at first were data entry to catch up on Medicare insurance filings. Without submitted claims, the company had no chance of recouping their costs and making a viable profit.

After just a few weeks on the job, Craig gave me more responsibilities. With those increased duties came raises, which prepared me financially for the impending separation and divorce from my husband. I knew that my Heavenly Father was looking out for my young family and me, and I was tremendously grateful.

My marriage continued to crumble until the day it ended, but instead of wondering where I was going to work or how I would provide for my family, I already had a good, challenging job that I enjoyed and which provided opportunities for further advancement.

Shortly after my divorce, Craig sent me on a business trip to Las Vegas to attend a medical conference where Medicare would present their new claim-filing structure. Since 95 percent of our billing was to Medicare, we needed to understand their new policies and procedures to ensure the future of the company. This massive assignment potentially had multi-million-dollar implications.

I had never traveled alone before to a destination where no one was expecting me. Plus, because of my recent divorce, I had no credit card and not a ton of cash to help me feel secure traveling.

In fact, before he left, my first husband had racked up all of our previous credit card accounts to their limit and then left the country without paying the debts. Not only was my credit trashed, but I was also forced to file bankruptcy to avoid the creditors who were after me for repayment of his debts.

Thankfully, my father arranged for me to get a credit card for emergencies through his business, and my company agreed to give me an advance to cover my expenses while I traveled.

Throughout this process, I prayed all along the way to be guided as I made plans to travel, as I boarded the plane to Las Vegas, and especially when I landed and headed to the conference. Not only was traveling alone foreign to me, but I also felt inadequate in the assignment.

I wasn't positive what information I needed to gather. I prayed as I looked through the conference schedule to know what breakout sessions to attend. I prayed as I went to the breakout sessions to understand what they were talking about. I prayed that I would be led to the right information that would allow me to go back to my company in Florida and report with accurate and correct information so that my trip would be deemed a success and I would have effectively accomplished what they sent me to accomplish.

My prayers were answered, and God led me every step of the way. I miraculously discovered the key components that we needed to know as a company to ensure financial viability.

More important, I now knew I could do hard things. I felt a sense of confidence that I could face anything with God's help and be effective. In just a couple of years, I had divorced, become a single mother with three kids, navigated a fruitful career, practiced faith in God to lead the way, and maintained a confidence and a sense of self that would have been impossible without the truth that my Heavenly Father inspired me with each and every day.

A few months after my trip to Las Vegas, my company sent me to their satellite office in New Jersey to audit their operations there. Again, I felt unsure and unprepared for the assignment.

I flew into Newark airport, rented a car, and drove to the office in a small town two hours west. I had never been to New Jersey, and it probably was the first time I rented a car as well. This was long before GPS was a useful navigation tool, so with map in hand, I made my way across the state, taking in the sights and smells of the northeast, driving along the imposingly large highway through Newark and then the wooded countryside, and finally arriving in a quaint town of red-bricked homes and open spaces.

Excited to have found the office so easily, I walked through the doors with a lively "hello!"

I was ready to introduce myself and get started, but the women leaning over their work at their desks raised their eyes with suspicion, and without lifting their heads, offered a quiet, "Hi." Their dubious expressions were not the greeting I was expecting. It hadn't occurred to me that they might resent my visit.

The New Jersey operation was run by the president and CEO's sister-in-law, Rebecca. One of her assistants led me back to her, and we discussed the plans for the two days I would be there. She matter-of-factly explained their processes and showed me their books where they were tracking their work.

"So how do you like working here?" I asked, attempting to break the ice and knowing that the satellite office was a new business in town.

"It's good," Rebecca replied. "It's a small town, so good jobs are not easy to find here. Everyone appreciates the work." We discussed the forming of the business there and how her brother-in-law had recruited her to start and develop the office.

"What did you do before?" I asked.

"I taught school."

"Oh, that's great. I always wanted to be a teacher. I actually studied education in college, and I love to teach," I said warming up to Rebecca and hoping she was warming up to me.

Once we had found some things in common and had enjoyed some friendly conversation, we were ready to get to work with greater trust and understanding.

The next two days raced by as we dug into the records. I collected valuable information about their processes and procedures, and I prepared to travel back to our main office to share what I had learned and offer recommendations for smoother transactions between our two locations.

Before I left, Rebecca brought me three of her favorite children's books from her collection as a teacher to bring back to my six-year-old daughter. I smiled at the friendship we had formed so quickly and her thoughtfulness in giving me these books.

Once again, with a map and written directions, I started the long drive from rural New Jersey to the busy Newark Airport. The directions to the city were clear, but the directions on how to get to the rental car return were not clear. A couple of hours later, I entered the city with its web of highways, once again praying to find my way.

Traffic was heavy during rush hour, and I hoped I had allowed enough time to make my flight since many arteries of the freeway were jammed with cars. Thankfully, the traffic was moving briskly in the direction I needed to go, but suddenly I realized that I had missed an exit.

As I drove past the exit, I noticed the cars were lined up bumper to bumper on the exit ramp. They didn't appear to be moving at all. I had no choice but to continue the direction I was going. I soon found myself driving into the airport and directly to the rental car return center. Had I exited where I thought I was supposed to, I would have been stuck in a bottleneck of traffic and possibly missed my flight. Instead, once again, I was led to the correct path and miraculously found my way.

These little miracles are what make life sweet. Recognizing that I can depend on God to lead me every step of the way when I make the effort and do my part is a beautiful assurance I love to remember in this messy life.

When I was drowning in my grief after my children's death, I relied on remembering these moments and others like them, the moments and experiences when I could not deny that my Heavenly Father was aware of me and was leading me as a young mother leads her toddler tenderly by the hand into new environments.

He could and would show me the way, and I could feel the tiniest reassurance that he could do so again. This time my experiences were more painful and challenging, but I could, ever so faintly, feel him offering his hand as I tried to adjust to my new circumstances—circumstances that included not having Carrie and David in our home and living with the painful reality that I had been the cause of their passing into the next realm.

Dallin, Carrie, Ron, James, and David
Yellowstone vacation 2005, Florida

CHAPTER 5

God Prepares Us

The darker the night, the brighter the stars,
The deeper the grief, the closer is God![1]

—Fyodor Dostoevsky

*I*n the weeks leading up to Carrie's and David's deaths, I had several unusual experiences that made no sense to me at the time. I didn't know it then, but these experiences contained powerful lessons that would sustain me after the accident.

About six weeks before Carrie and David died, I traveled with my friend JoLynn, her husband, and a couple of other friends from Houston to a conference in Kansas City. JoLynn had a good friend, June, who had moved from Spring, Texas, to Kansas a couple of years earlier. June had lost her seventeen-year-old daughter in a freak accident six years before, and JoLynn had actively supported her after her daughter's death.

JoLynn spent a couple of days with June while we were there. As we drove home, she shared some of the experiences she had with June over the weekend, including June's renewed capacity.

Like so many grieving parents, after her daughter's death, June experienced a period of immense mourning, adjustment, and healing. The days had been long and hard. Now June was rebuilding her life. She was again actively involved in church service, working as a nurse, and participating enthusiastically in her other children's lives.

After my accident, remembering JoLynn's retelling of June's experience strengthened my resolve that I could rebuild my life too.

In addition, other stories of mothers who had lost children were shared that day on the road. As I listened, I could not imagine how you could survive such a tragedy. My heart ached for these mothers whose children became sick and died, or the mother whose child was unintentionally left in a suffocating car, or the parents whose child died in a freak accident. Even the very thought of it was too much to bear. *What is left after such a dreadful loss? How could anyone bear that amount of agony?*

During this same ride home, there was a discussion about the power of the devil. As I listened, a deep sense of testimony of God's power washed over me, burning in my heart. I remembered a verse in the scriptures I had studied about the Lord's great power, and I felt compelled to share the verse and my conviction that God's power is always greater than any negative influence in the world.

The King of Syria was fighting against Israel, but the prophet Elisha received the Syrian king's plot by revelation from God, which he sent to the King of Israel. The King of Syria became aware that Elisha the prophet was thwarting his plans against Israel, so he sent his army in the darkness of night to surround and surprise the city of Dothan where Elisha stayed.

The next morning, Elisha's servant went to the window and saw the frightening view of soldiers, chariots, and horses encompassing the city. In terror, his servant said to Elisha, "Alas, my master! how shall we do?" (2 Kings 6:15).

Elisha answered him, "Fear not: for they that be with us are more than they that be with them" (2 Kings 6:16). Then Elisha prayed that his servant's eyes would be open to see the truth: "'I pray thee, open his eyes, that he may see.' And the Lord opened the eyes of the young man; and he saw: and, behold, the mountain was full of horses and chariots of fire round about Elisha" (2 Kings 6:17).

"They that be with us are more than they that be with them" was and is a compelling reminder of God's power and influence in my own life. My circumstances are different. I'm not fighting an army and facing soldiers and chariots, but remembering that God's power is greater than any evil and shadowy darkness on earth is comforting as I navigate my challenges.

After the accident, remembering this powerful spiritual enlightening of the greatness of the power of God helped me further understand that if my children weren't meant to die so young, they would still be here. Similarly, if the Spirit can whisper in my ear to bring my arm in, surely, that same Spirit could have warned me that I was sleepy and prevented the accident from happening at all.

Still, I could not accept this idea fully into my heart, even with all the evidence before me. My heart was aching with longing for Carrie and David to still be with us in our home, playing on the trampoline, swimming in the pool, and filling the air with their laughter and joy.

While we were cleaning out Carrie's room, I found her scripture bag. Tucked in her scriptures was a church program on which she had drawn a picture of a girl with "Carrie" written above it. An arrow pointed to a drawing of a man with "Jesus" written above it. Her drawing foreshadowed her return home to Him.

Also folded in her bag was an envelope. I opened the envelope to a note that said, "My gift to Jesus is love." Both of these items brought solace to my aching heart. I knew God had prepared Carrie to return to her heavenly home, and I knew she was still blessing us with her love.

For several months after the accident, I would see things and want to share it with Carrie and David, only to remember that they were no longer there. I would see a cute stuffed animal and think, *Carrie would love this adorable pink, fluffy dog.* I would see a park and think, *I should bring David here to play one day.* These thoughts would be followed by the shocking realization that I could not share these things with them anymore.

One day in September, I walked into a Walgreens and noticed the Halloween costumes they had just put out on the racks. I saw a flowing, black witch costume with a touch of red accents, and I immediately thought, *This is perfect for Carrie. She would love this.* Again, the shock overcame me with the present truth that I would not need a costume for Carrie this year or any year after.

Why did this have to happen? Why is she not here with me? I lamented immediately, sinking back into the dark gloom that was the constant of my days.

And then I heard a voice in my head: *She's right where she's supposed to be.* I immediately knew I was being reminded that things were as they should be, even if I despised Carrie's and David's absence.

If this is how it's supposed to be, why did it have to happen like that? Why did I have to be driving the car?

And the answer came tenderly, *How would you have liked for it to happen?*

My mind scanned and searched for a good response, but there was none.

No alternative way existed for my children to die that wouldn't have been equally devastating. No escape existed for the desperate pain of a parent's aching heart after the death of her children, no matter the circumstances of their death.

Five years before, they had both fallen out the second-floor window of our home in a freak accident. We had just come home from visiting friends. Carrie and David went upstairs to the second floor playroom. It was a spring day, and they opened the window to shout to the dog in the back yard. They both leaned on the screen of the opened window. The screen suddenly gave way, and they fell to the pool deck below.

We rushed them to the hospital. We were frantic with worry, but fortunately, they only sustained minor injuries. David hardly had a scratch and was released after being examined. Carrie had minor fractures in both wrists and was bruised. She wore two pink casts for a few weeks but recovered fully.

My mother has said that it was this freak accident when they were five and three that really helped her know that they were meant to go together. We were grateful to have them here for another five years.

In April, the month before our tragic accident, Heather, a thirty-year-old wife and mother from church, lost her battle with cancer. She discovered she was pregnant and was diagnosed with cancer shortly afterward. Because of her pregnancy, her cancer treatments were modified to protect the baby. Eventually, the baby was developed enough that the doctor's induced labor. Unfortunately, Heather died two weeks later.

I was asked to play the organ for the funeral, but I was feeling unusually emotional, which I thought was from the recent anniversary of my brother's death, and I declined to play. Now I believe that the emotions I felt that month were anticipation of my loss that would occur the next month.

That may seem unusual, but I do believe that our spirits know more about our past, present, and future than we realize. I believe the foreboding I experienced during the six weeks before Carrie's and David's deaths came from an inner knowing of what was to come.

I attended Heather's funeral, and as I walked into the viewing and saw her husband standing at the foot of her coffin, I was overcome with an inspired vision of God's love for this good man.

I barely knew him. He was a young widower with two small boys and an infant baby girl. I know his heart was broken, but I felt God's compassion and great love for him.

I also felt a tremendous sense of God's trust in this young husband and father to carry on, despite the devastating loss of his wife and the mother of his children. God knew his heart and knew that he would be faithful and righteous and would raise his kids in love and virtue.

, Of all my experiences leading up to Carrie's and David's deaths, this was the most unusual. I hardly knew this young man. In fact, I'm not sure I ever even had a conversation with him before that day. Why would Heavenly Father give me such a vision of his love and trust in this young father?

I reflected on this encounter many times after losing my kids. Maybe God loved me too despite my challenges. Maybe he was giving me a glimpse of the love and trust he had in me. Maybe he was reminding me, as he reminded Job, that my loss had nothing to do with my worthiness for his love.

Even though I felt so much pain each day, these visions of trust, of the confirming testimony of God's power in this world, of the evidence of hope of recovery and of the whispering of the Spirit that reminded me of God's will, provided evidence that I had been prepared for this tragedy and that I was being patiently guided through my grief.

————

NOTE

1. Fyodor Dostoevsky, *Crime and Punishment* (Mineola, NY: Dover Publications, 2001). See reddit.com/r/dostoevsky/comments/doh57h/the_darker_ the_night_the_brighter_the_stars_the/. Accessed June 3, 2020.

CHAPTER 6

Healing Comfort

Blessed be God . . . who comforteth us in all our tribulation,
that we may be able to comfort them which are in any trouble,
by the comfort wherewith we ourselves are comforted by God.

—2 Corinthians 1:3–4

As I think of my healing, I think of loving family, friends, and professionals who were willing to sustain me in my pain.

Immediately after the accident, my world shrank and became dark and distressing. I spent many days lying in bed in a painful haze, unable to think or sleep.

In a world that enjoys finding a culprit to blame, I was terribly aware that I was solely responsible for what had happened. How could I do this to my family? How could I do this to Ron, who held a deep love for his children? What could I have done differently? Surely, there was something I could have done to keep this heartbreak from happening.

There were no answers, only questions. There was no solace, only discomfort. There was no relief, only anxiety and deep despair.

Sensing my collapse, my sister Kari rearranged her summer plans, and she and her ten-year-old son, Chase, stayed at our house for weeks. She willingly sat with me and listened. She coordinated helpers and ran interference when necessary. She took care of everything that didn't require Ron or me.

My mother also came and stayed. We worked on thank you cards together, and my sister and mother attempted to keep me occupied and moving. They helped us care for James, and they got me to doctor's appointments when Ron wasn't available. They literally became the light in our home.

Our tragedy was like an earthquake with seismic waves that rippled out from the epicenter. In an earthquake, the further the waves travel the less damaging they are. However, those closest or at the epicenter of the tragedy are immediately impacted, and they sustain the most lasting damage. They may be injured and their homes destroyed. It takes time, effort, and attention for them to recover from the harm done by the earthquake. As you move further away from the epicenter, there's less damage, less personal injury, and less devastation.

Those farthest away feel the effects as minor tremors. They may faintly hear the doors rattling or the china clinking in the cabinets, but once the earthquake is over, it hasn't changed anything for them.

They dress the next morning, take their kids to school, drive to work, and after work, they stop at the grocery store on the way home for milk, bread, and cereal. Their day-to-day lives are unchanged.

Those on the edges of the tremor are unaware of the difficulties those at the epicenter are facing. They are so absorbed in their day-to-day that they don't recognize the blessing of mundane activities. For them, life goes on as normal, and they simply cannot be expected to understand the impact of the damage at the epicenter.

My husband, our kids, and I were at the epicenter of tragedy. Our lives were unrecognizable. We lived in emotional rubble. The damage was great, and rebuilding was a fuzzy idea so far off in the distance that it was distorted and felt improbable, if not impossible.

Our closest family, including my sister and my mother, were right outside of the epicenter of damage. They were close enough so that they felt the enormous pain and witnessed the destruction, but far enough outside of the ring of devastation that they were able to come to our assistance.

They were able to start the cleanup effort, to begin to pull us from the rubble, to brush the debris from our clothes, and to wipe the grime from our dirty faces. They were our loving first responders.

Our friends felt the rumble of the tragedy and came to our aid as well, including my husband's boss and coworkers. Typically, Ron's work at the time as a technology strategist for Microsoft ramped up significantly during May and June. He would work long hours in those months to finalize their contracts with their corporate clients before the end of the fiscal year on June 30th.

In May 2007, he should have been in his busiest season of the year, which would have meant long hours and tremendous stress to meet his deadlines. Instead, in May 2007, before Mother's Day, the accounts for which he was responsible had already closed their deals with record sales.

Because the contract work was complete, Ron's boss told him to stay home and take care of his family. He didn't return to work full time until July—another miracle that blessed our lives. Even though our lives were decimated, I could see God's goodness.

Friends showed up on our doorstep just wanting to help with the dishes, meals, and other household chores, or to just sit in silent comfort and support. Many sat on the edge of my bed, on the floor, or on the chair in my bedroom and quietly offered their strength. My heart is astounded by the unassuming love that was shared with my family and me.

I recognize that not everyone has this level of support. Even in my other struggles in life, I've never seen such an outpouring of pure love and concern. Certain tragedies engender different types of support, depending on the circumstances.

Some trials are not as public or as sudden. In general, people are not prepared to help us in grief. Grief makes people uncomfortable, and it's sad that we've been taught to leave people alone and let them have their space. When situations develop over time (like a divorce) instead of suddenly, people tend to wonder when it's appropriate to interject themselves, but giving people space is an unfortunate myth that helps no one.

People need people. Buddha said, "In separateness lies the world's great misery; in compassion lies the world's true strength." We need a compassionate witness. I needed compassionate witnesses.[1]

Ron and I struggled. We knew very little about grief. Even though we both had experienced it in the past, we were still operating with incorrect information and few tools to help us.

Because we were living through the same loss, I believed we would grieve together or that our grief would look and feel the same. In the beginning days, it did. Ron comforted me as I recovered from my physical wounds, but eventually, he needed to care for his own.

While we both lost Carrie and David, our losses were different. We both longed for Carrie and David to still be with us, but our grief was as different as our relationships were with each child and as different as our involvement in the accident.

I remember my mom telling me once how lucky I was to have Carrie in the middle of my three sons. She expressed how fortunate I was to have this younger daughter as a companion as my family grew up and my older two daughters left home. I agreed with her, and Carrie was the perfect youngest daughter—loving, kind, and anxious to please. Now she was gone, and I didn't feel very lucky anymore.

I had been homeschooling Carrie and David. Carrie was compliant and happy to learn, but she and David both suffered from dyslexia, and learning to read was a struggle. David, on the other hand, was an active boy and not as eager to sit to read and write. My mother-in-law often commented that his spirit was too big for his body and that's why he was so overactive. She may have been right, because while he was a handful to teach, he had a heart of gold that was bigger than all of Texas.

On Carrie's ninth birthday, we had a pool party for her and all her girlfriends. One by one, she opened the many gifts her friends brought her, including a set of twin baby dolls. When we gathered the girls to take a picture by the pool, David wandered into the picture, with a doll in his arms and holding a bottle to its molded lips. He was so preoccupied in loving his baby that he didn't even notice he was getting in the way of the camera.

Years later, we still enjoy our David stories. In fact, we're convinced that our boy inspired the picture book *No, David!* One Saturday morning, David disappeared. I thought he was upstairs playing until he came through the door with a party favor. He had snuck out of the house to ride his bike early in the morning and came across a party for a neighbor child who was twice his age. He immediately invited himself to the party. He crept back into our house, grabbed a toy, and wrapped it to take back to the party that he crashed. We were amazed at his audacity.

One day I was taking his sister to piano lessons and David insisted on staying home. He was watching a cartoon, and I gave him specific instructions to stay on the couch while I was gone and to keep the doors locked. Five minutes later when I returned, David was in the garage with our elderly neighbor, looking for a ladder. He had locked himself out of the house and decided he needed a ladder to get in an upstairs window.

When David was a preschooler, the older kids, Carrie, James, and Dallin, were sitting around the dining room table for their morning homeschool lessons when Carrie looked up and noticed water dripping from the chandelier. I ran upstairs to catch David soaking towels in the sink and placing them in the middle of the floor, which eventually soaked all the way through the floor and the ceiling and dripped from the chandelier. Of course, he didn't have an explanation as to why he was doing it. He was always exploring and trying new things at my absolute exasperation.

There was never an end to his mischief. I wondered how old he would be when he was finally grown up. He created a brown sugar trail up the stairs and to his closet, smashed banana into his sister's pillow, hung linking toys to the balcony for "bungee jumping," painted the pool deck with his brother's model paints, and filled our lives with fun and laughter. With David around, drawers and closets were emptied onto the floor, wallpaper was peeled from the walls, nothing stayed in order, and his bright smile made our hearts burst with love.

Ron's relationship with David was unique. I often reminded Ron that he was David's dad not his grandpa, because Ron had an easygoing, laid-back enjoyment of everything David did. Ron enjoyed watching and coaching David's baseball, soccer, and basketball teams. Nothing he did was annoying or too much in Ron's eyes. It was all pure fun.

Carrie was Ron's Care Bear and frequent companion. If he had an errand to run, he took one of the kids with him. Ron made it easier for me to homeschool, because when he was home, he was a hands-on dad, helping them with the pinewood derby cars, taking them shopping for what they needed, or inviting them along on grocery trips. He loved these kids to the moon and back, and no one ever doubted his complete delight in all his children.

I attended a book club a few years ago, and the novel we discussed was *The Snow Child*, based on the Russian fairy-tale "The Snow Maiden." The story goes that an elderly couple, who were never able to have children of their own, decided to make a snow child who came to life. For as the wife says to her husband, "Better to make a snow-child, since Heaven will not grant us a live one."

In the novel, the couple's relationship was strained because of their grief over never having a child. The husband and wife had their own ways of dealing with the grief, and they struggled to come together to comfort one another. During our discussion at book club, several comments were made about how odd it was that the husband and wife suffered alone and didn't find some way of supporting one another in their grief.

On the other hand, I understood the novel's point of view, but I could also see how this would be strange to an outside observer. Having gone through tragedy with Ron, I knew how difficult it is to support one another when you each are equally in need of comfort. My aunt explained it best when she compared it to two people suffering in two hospital beds next to each other. You know the other is suffering but you are incapacitated to help.

I was so consumed with self-reproach that I rejected any attempts of soothing. I was in no position to comfort another, and witnessing Ron's pain only increased my self-hatred. After all, I was to blame for our suffering. Ron was so burdened with his heavy grief that while he tried to reassure me, he was doing well to survive minute by minute. We were wholly unable to help each other.

Typically, men tend to grieve in stoic silence, choosing to bury themselves in their work, while women are more vocal and expressive with their grief. This is a broad generalization, but we found this to be mostly true in our relationship.

To add to the problem, one spouse may feel that their way is the right way to grieve and assume their husband or wife is doing it wrong, so they pressure their partner to change their style of grief. Granted, while true understanding of grief and healing and the tools that support healing are helpful, there is no one way to grieve.

I've learned over time that patience and understanding and a willingness to be a compassionate witness are more encouraging than judgmental expectations. Unfortunately, I didn't understand this while I was in it, and I know I pressured Ron to grieve and show up in specific ways that were not helpful to him.

After the accident, we met with our bishop, who expressed his concern for us and our relationship. I told him I didn't know how our marriage would survive, because the odds were against us. This was the second marriage for both of us. Second marriages have a higher divorce rate, and losing our children further increased our odds of separation.

The bishop responded, "We are not going to let that happen." As sweet as his encouragement was, I doubted his ability to keep that promise.

If we think about the hospital scenario, your roommate does not help you heal. It's the nurses, attendants, and doctors.

I'm grateful that while Ron and I lay parallel and paralyzed, suffering in our metaphorical hospital beds, we had good friends and family that took care of us until we could take care of ourselves.

Eventually, Ron and I sought professional help from a therapist. We met a couple of times for marriage counseling, but eventually our therapist suggested that I needed to work on my heavy guilt, complicated grief, and PTSD symptoms. I started going to see her regularly, and she gently led me through weeks of talk therapy and EMDR. Not only did it help me let go of my extreme guilt and navigate my new life, it also eventually helped me with my severe fear of driving a car or even being a passenger.

Marriage counseling was plainly not what we needed at that time since we were so engrossed in our individual pain that it was impossible to see things clearly. Our irritation toward one another was laced with our hurt. Releasing the hurt did more to help our marriage than anything. Working on my individual issues allowed me to start my healing process. I believe when the individuals in a couple are whole, so is the marriage.

I'm convinced that if not for Ron's compassionate heart, we would not be married today. His willingness to forgive me and stick by me through those bleak days is remarkable to me. I felt like a burden. I wanted to leave and never return, and I pushed him away in significant ways. He was always calmly patient with my grief, even when I didn't return the same to him. Eventually we made our way through and learned to not only survive together, but also to thrive despite unimaginable trials.

———

NOTE

1. See goodreads.com/quotes/33079-in-separateness-lies-the-world-s-greatest-misery-in-compassion-lies. Accessed June 3, 2020.

CHAPTER 7

Being Strong

Numbing the pain for a while will make
it worse when you finally feel it.[1]

—Dumbledore

*R*on made appointments for our family to see a counselor a couple of weeks after the accident. So much of the burden of keeping things together had fallen on him, and I'm sure he was looking for someone who could help him deal with all the heavy emotions in our house. Stephanie was back at college, but within days, the rest of us, Ron and I, Kristin, Dallin, and James, went to see a therapist we had never met.

We entered the waiting room in a solemn stupor, none of us talking to the other. I doubt we even gave our kids a proper explanation as to what to expect, most likely because we didn't know either. We had scheduled the appointment with so little notice that they fit us all into an extended evening appointment. The black night sky outside matched my feelings as the receptionist ushered us into a side room.

First, the therapist met with each of our children individually, talking to them about what happened and their feelings about it. While he met with them, Ron and I waited in a small, bare office with nothing except a handful of metal chairs scattered throughout.

After his brief meeting with each of our kids, he met with Ron and me. I sat quietly, again behind dark glasses, holding my casted arm across me as protection. I didn't want to be there as he explained the impact this event would have on our family. I felt the burden of our loss every moment of every sad day, and I couldn't bear to consider the long-term ramifications.

He explained that our strong emotions of grief and pain could manifest in unkind comments and actions toward each other. He said we should expect that and try to identify it as just a symptom of our grief, so we didn't put undo meaning on these painful interactions.

He further recommended that we create a term to use to identify when our actions were due to the accident and not truly attached to the current circumstances. For example, we could call our grief or the accident "the box," and if I overreacted, I could label it "the box" to explain my behavior to the family. That way we could give each other some additional leeway for overreactions and heightened emotions.

My ears perked up as he warned us that it was normal to have crazy thoughts as our minds tried to assimilate the changes. This bit of information was particularly helpful to me since my thoughts had been increasingly bizarre. It was as if I was living in a fun house where everything in my surroundings was distorted. My mind would ping-pong from one unusual thought to another, never really landing on anything that made sense.

I don't recall saying more than a couple of sentences during the entire exchange, but as I sat there with my cast on my arm and my eyes still blackened from the impact of the crash, he turned to me, looked me in the eye, and said, "You look like a strong woman. You can choose to be happy."

I had no verbal response, but I thought, *You don't even know me.*

We made no specific plans to go back. We returned home with a few tidbits of information and tried to tape our lives back together as best we could. What were we thinking? That somehow one visit would heal our hearts?

Eventually, as I mentioned before, Ron and I sought regular marriage counseling that quickly evolved into me in individual therapy.

Grief was like the waves of the ocean that crashed incessantly upon me. Before I could recover from the previous wave, another would collapse over me. Just as I was reaching my feet to the sand below, much less standing up, another wave would knock me down. I was out of breath and weary.

Somehow as I fought to raise my head above the foamy water, I still had a faint hope that life could get better, that I could survive and somehow enjoy my life again.

The words of the first therapist rang in my head. "You look like a strong woman. You can choose to be happy." Fortunately, I knew enough about grief to know that relief from the pain was not going to happen instantaneously. I remembered what it was like to lose my brother and to feel that heavy sadness for months. I knew to be patient with myself, to not expect much from myself, and to be still for a season.

Each time I would feel myself become impatient in those first few months, I would remind myself to lower my expectations. *Lay low. Give yourself space and time*, I told myself.

Friends would often tell me how great I was doing. I didn't feel great, and I wasn't sure what they were referring to, but I think because I wasn't a wailing heap on the floor every time I saw them, I looked like I was doing pretty good. Nevertheless, inside I was imploding.

In December, Ron interviewed for a possible job transfer from Houston to Salt Lake City. He came home from work enthusiastic about the opportunity. "This is just what we need," he said. "A new start."

Salt Lake City would put us closer to our girls who were both attending school in Idaho by this time, but I would be far from my friends who were supporting me, who were holding my hand through the grief, and who were willing to talk about Carrie and David. Plus, Carrie and David were buried right there a few miles from our house, and we just put the fresh gravestone down to mark their grave. If I moved to Utah, no one there would know my kids. Ever. I would leave behind everything I currently knew.

Moving is hard enough, but moving with fresh grief in my heart was an unbearable thought. Sure, we would also be leaving behind the visual triggers, including their bedrooms where they had played and slept, the parks they had played in, the trampoline in the back corner of the yard where they had jumped for hours, our backyard pool that they had swam in, and the friends they had loved.

Moving away from those triggers may have been easier in some ways, but they were also the cues each day that validated Carrie and David's very existence. Without those cues and our friends, we would be instantly losing the memories. Not that Carrie and David would slip from our memory, but they would not exist in our new world.

Ron was adamant that this was the best route for our family. I went to bed, the burden too heavy to bear. What little progress I had made unraveled with the prospect of moving. I was unable to function, and so my bed was my respite. I searched for the strength to follow his passion, but I couldn't get there.

That's when I introduced the idea of marriage therapy. I thought a neutral party could assist us in coming to a mutually beneficial conclusion, but before we even got to our first appointment, Ron rejected the job opportunity. We weren't moving to Salt Lake City. I should have been happy, but the decision became another burden to me as I felt myself standing between Ron and this new career prospect.

I had learned years before that making major changes during the first year after a devastating loss was unwise. All major decisions and changes should be put off. This was one of the rules as I understood them. Surely, we shouldn't move in the first year. Major changes could be due to the rebound effect and have grave consequences or result in severe regrets later. Right or wrong, I held to this "rule"—no major changes in the first year.

I was certain that no matter where we ended up, we would be bringing our burdens with us. Our grief would not have stayed in Houston. Even in new surroundings, we would still be mourning our beautiful children. We would still need love and support from family and friends.

To this day, I don't know if moving would have worked out well for us. It would have been what it was—a decision. We decided to stay, so that became the best decision for us, because it was the decision we made.

I've learned it's not valid to compare the outcome of a choice we made with the unknown outcome of a choice we didn't make. Invariably when we have regrets, we look at the option we turned down and assume incorrectly that it would have turned out perfectly. We create an unrealistically pretty picture to accompany the unmade choice and compare it to the way things turned out. It's an inaccurate equation and is never useful.

Ron and I continued to struggle, mostly because I was struggling, and the Salt Lake City opportunity became another brick in our wall. Life was hard and unpleasant. There was no joy. There was no light.

I blamed myself for every difficulty in our life, including turning down the Utah job. If Ron was stressed, it was my fault. If the kids were struggling, it was my fault. That's how I viewed my world.

Week after week, I walked into the counselor's office with barely any perceptible improvement. Each week I waited in her waiting room, wondering what we were going to accomplish today. She would come out to gather me from the waiting room, and I towered over her petite frame as I followed her back to her office.

She sat in a straight-back chair across from where I sat on the proverbial couch, which was under a window and facing the door. Her desk was off to the left from my view, and she had a few plants and pictures to decorate the space, plus a small tabletop water feature to add some white noise. My mental vision was so cloudy that even now when I recall my visits, the room seems dim and hazy.

Unlike my visit to the first therapist, she rarely added too much to the conversation, mostly asking me questions and listening for my responses. Each week I expressed how miserable I was, and while I saw a glimmer of hope far off in the future, it was hard to imagine what that would look like in reality. She listened intently with a therapist's stoicism while revealing the slightest unconcealed empathy and concern on her face.

Week after week, we had the same conversation as I expressed in my weak, sad demeanor that I didn't know what to do, where to go, or how to heal. She gave me occasional assignments, which I rarely did.

For nearly two years, we repeated this pattern, and slowly I started to reengage in life in small ways.

When my shoulders and wrists were healed, I rejoined my tennis team that I had joined at the beginning of 2007. Tennis was another tender mercy from the Lord.

My tennis friends remained kind and supportive. They attended the funeral. They brought meals to our family. They encouraged me to participate at whatever level I felt comfortable. As soon as I was able, I started playing again.

I enjoyed the distraction from my thoughts and the drudgery of my life. On the court, I could focus on one fuzzy yellow ball and forget everything else. We worked as a team, and there was a sense of camaraderie that was uplifting and beneficial.

After a match or practice, we would sit in the shade under the large oak trees that covered the decks next to the courts. I enjoyed the warm friendships and listened to their lively chatter of ordinary family life while the sun glinted through the branches, the breeze softly rustled the trees, and birds chirped overhead—an idyllic scene for healing.

Before the accident, all eight of us were home, until Stephanie went back to college in April. We had a full house. Kristin was a senior in high school, and I homeschooled Dallin, James, Carrie, and David with Stephanie's help.

I also led our local homeschool group, which included over forty families, weekly education days, regular teen activities, and monthly parent support meetings. The teen group and parent group often met in our home or at our neighborhood clubhouse down the street. Life was full.

After the accident, Stephanie went back to college. Kristin graduated from high school two weeks later and left soon after for a summer outdoor theater experience in New York before heading to college that fall. Within weeks, we went from eight at home to four.

One quiet summer day, I sat in my home office by the front door of our home. Dallin came in and sat on the wood floor next to my chair. He laid his head gently on my knee as he tearfully shared, "I miss jumping on the trampoline with Carrie and David." We tenderly cried together.

The many shared daily activities had been the joys of homeschooling the kids. We were all hurting. Life would never be the same.

I had been involved in homeschooling for eleven years. We started when Stephanie and Kristin were in third and first grade respectively. After our first year, we moved to Dallas, where we found an active eclectic homeschool community.

We always had many activities to choose from. In Dallas, we went to numerous daytime plays, symphony performances, and the opera. We participated in field trips to the zoo and the museums in Dallas and Fort Worth.

Our local group created Destination Imagination groups, which Stephanie, Kristin, Dallin, and James joined. Destination Imagination is a creative contest where teams from local schools compete in demonstrating problem solving and presentation skills. Each year a new challenge is introduced, and the student teams work on solving the problem and presenting their solution in an entertaining format. It's a hands-on, student-led experience, supported by teachers and, in our case, parents.

The girls especially loved singing in a homeschool choir. Mary, one of the moms in our group, sang for the Dallas Opera Company, and she put on a choir class each year that culminated in a themed musical performance at the end of the semester. She offered each student a solo part if they wanted one. Stephanie and Kristin gained so much confidence from participating in her choir.

On the second day I brought Kristin to the class, I noticed the director was behind the piano trying to lead the group and pound out the notes. Afterward, I asked if I could help. I told Mary I would love to be her practice pianist if that would be helpful. She accepted my offer. Another friend helped watch my younger kids, including two-year-old David, on the playground while I accompanied the choir's practices.

When Stephanie turned fourteen, she wanted to go back to public school to compete with the swim team. Because of some unusual regulations with the school, it didn't work out for her to attend the local high school in Dallas her freshman year. She was crushed, and I was crushed for her. I wondered if I could have done something differently to make the transition work.

About this time, a friend was starting a charter school near our house. We went to some of the parent meetings and decided to enroll our four oldest in ninth, seventh, fourth, and first grades at the new school. School started, and unfortunately, Ron's work ended. It was the beginning of the tech bubble burst, and the company he worked for went under.

Then just two weeks into the new school year, terrorists attacked New York and Washington on 9-11. The whole world seemed to stop for weeks after, but by Thanksgiving that year, Ron accepted a job with Microsoft. We sold our house in Dallas and started our move to Spring, Texas, north of Houston.

Again, God had our best interest in his hands. Because the public high school in Dallas had been on an unusual block schedule, Stephanie's transition to the high school in Spring would have been nearly impossible because of the different structure. She would have needed to stay in Dallas for six months to finish out the school year.

Instead, because she was at the charter school, whose schedule synced with her new high school, she was able to join us in just three weeks after the fall semester ended. Again, I was so grateful that even in our disappointment, all had worked out as it should. Once again, I was reminded of how God knows our needs even before we do.

We moved to Spring, and Stephanie joined the swim team at her new high school. All the kids transferred from the charter school in Dallas to the local public schools in Spring and finished out the school year. The following year, Dallin and James returned to homeschooling, Stephanie continued at the high school, and Kristin attended the middle school.

The four younger children and I quickly became involved in a homeschool group again. As my children got a little older, I did increasingly more volunteering in our group, even helping with a homeschool conference and speaking at homeschool events.

By this time, I had been homeschooling for many years, and I assumed that I would always be involved with it even after my kids were grown. I enjoyed going to various homeschool conferences, and I observed vendors who supported the homeschooling community. I even had a friend who had homeschooled her kids until they were grown and then helped homeschool her grandchildren. She also continued to speak at homeschool events. This seemed ideal.

I loved homeschooling my children. I loved the shared experiences and watching them learn and grow together. I also loved watching the close bonds my children developed with each other because of their mutual activities, but it wasn't always easy.

I was known for saying, "Homeschooling would be easy if it weren't for the kids." Certainly, the children were the variable in schooling them, but I had dreams of always being involved with the homeschool community, like my friend who was teaching her grandkids and supporting parents in their desire to teach their children.

When Carrie and David died, my interest in homeschooling faded away overnight. Homeschooling was another daily reminder of what we had lost. Dallin was fifteen and James was twelve, and I knew in my heart that sending them back to school after such a shocking loss would not be helpful.

I also felt inadequate to continue to teach them, so I leaned more on alternative options. We eventually found an online school that would administer their education and provide follow up and grading. Over time, I got more involved again in their education, and I even explored the idea of bringing other kids into our school to teach them as well. That idea fizzled out, but it was an indication that I was doing better.

Another way I attempted to reengage in life was regularly attending church services. From the beginning, I knew instinctively that I needed to be there. While I appreciated the messages shared and knew they were benefitting me, going to church was one of my most difficult outings each week.

Spiritual matters closely align with emotions, and my emotions were on overload. Intellectually I knew that church is for the sinner and the humble, not the saintly and perfect. However, when I was there, I felt a constant pull between appearing okay and not wanting to appear too okay. I was uncomfortably aware of how I was coming across to others.

If I acted like everything was okay even if I wasn't, then I would appear to not have loved my kids. If I showed up an emotional mess, people would think I was falling apart and emotionally unstable. Emotionally unstable was closer to my truth, but I wasn't prepared to announce that to the world. Every week included this inner struggle, but still, I showed up.

On occasion, my emotions would get the best of me, and I'd leave between services and Sunday School. One Sunday, I was too overcome to leave the bench, and I sat sobbing in the pew while the congregation filed out. A friend came over to comfort me, saying, "You're doing so good."

"I don't feel like I'm doing good," I cried, feeling completely inadequate.

"But you are," she insisted.

I was not convinced. The fact was, I had no idea how to navigate my heavy feelings. I had no tools to create some space in my mind. I had no tools to evaluate what I was thinking so I could reasonably make decisions about how I wanted to feel. In retrospect, in many ways I was doing good. I was showing up and figuring it out. That's really all I could ask of myself.

Haruki Murakami said, "Pain is inevitable, but suffering is optional."[2] I created so much suffering with my self-hatred. I was not nice to myself. I did not want to exist anymore. Living and breathing felt forced on me.

Each morning I would wake up wishing I hadn't. I wondered why I survived the accident. I concluded that everyone's life would have been far better had I died too. Of course, it wasn't true, but that was my thought process.

Eventually my patience with myself wore out, and my long-standing self-loathing took a toll. I could no longer tell myself that of course I'm not doing well. I wanted to be better. I demanded that I be better. Being strong sounded good on paper, but was an impossible proposition. I couldn't figure it out.

I remembered the instruction from the first therapist. "You look like a strong woman. You can choose to be happy."

You can choose to be happy, rang in my head repeatedly.

But I'm not happy. Why can't I choose to be happy? What am I doing wrong? These incessant worries plagued my thoughts. *Will this be my fate, to be in pain forever?*

I was trying! But even though I was attempting to reengage with life, nothing seemed to make things better. I was spending time with friends playing tennis, I was reengaged with my boys' schooling, I was going to church, but I felt horrible.

I had been patient with my grief in the beginning. I understood in the early stages that I was hurting and that the pain required patience to heal, but eventually my patience ran out.

Tragically, I used the statement "you can choose to be happy" against myself instead of for me. I berated myself for not being happy. It caused me to spiral down further. I was trying to power through my grief instead of patiently doing the work.

I spun in negativity, not knowing how to be happy, and then I assumed something was wrong with me because I couldn't figure it out. Over time, I became severely depressed.

My oldest daughter married in December 2007, just seven months after the accident. I was in no position to plan a wedding, so my friend Jennifer, who had helped with funeral preparations and who Stephanie had nannied for, asked if she could help.

Jennifer offered to host a reception at her beautiful home and planned everything. She shopped endlessly for the perfect decorations for the celebration. When she found something new, she would ask what I thought. I always agreed with every choice, because I trusted her flawless taste, and I didn't have the strength to care.

A couple of months before the wedding, Jennifer invited me to meet at her house to discuss the food for the reception. Shortly after I arrived, her friend Ellen showed up and joined us at the table. I had only briefly met Ellen once before and was surprised at her involvement in planning my daughter's wedding.

As Jennifer and Ellen discussed vegetable and fruit displays, cheese hors d'oeuvres, wedding cake and punch, I turned to Ellen and asked, "Why are you doing this?" I couldn't understand why someone would devote so much time and attention to helping a stranger with a wedding.

She replied simply, "I just want to help." I was stunned by her generosity. Putting on a wedding is not for wimps, and volunteering to help a stranger was incredible to me. I felt extremely humbled by her eagerness to serve.

Stephanie and her fiancé Chris lived in Idaho, where they were still attending college, so wedding preparation happened while they were away. Because they would marry in Houston, arriving just in time to get a marriage license and then return to Idaho for a celebration there, and because it was winter, we decided to do silk flowers. My friend Gloria offered to help shop and arrange flowers, including the bridal bouquet.

Yet another friend, Kelly, created the perfect wedding cake to Stephanie's specifications, and my family arrived early to help with set up. We were surrounded by friends and family who supported us in our pain and in our celebration. The many people who stepped up to help with the wedding were another example of people's goodness and God's grace in sending help.

Stephanie and Chris's wedding was beautiful because of generous hearts that saw a need and came to our aid once again. Unfortunately, my pain was deep, and I struggled to appreciate the beauty of the day.

After the wedding, family and friends returned to their routines, and Stephanie and Chris returned to Idaho. My life returned to a dismal slog.

Over the next year, I threw myself into exercise, sometimes spending two to three hours at the gym in addition to playing tennis several days a week. The physical exertion seemed to be the only relief from my emotional discomfort.

After the accident, I indulged in unbridled eating, which was easy to do with all the rich food coming into the house for months from friends who wanted to help. My activity level took the edge off my climbing weight until I eventually decided to do something about it.

When I was in college, I was diagnosed with Graves disease due to an overactive thyroid tumor. They removed most of my thyroid surgically, but in the following years, it grew back, and I underwent radiation on my thyroid to shrink the tumor. As a result, I no longer have a functioning thyroid. This condition has made it harder but not impossible to control my weight. However, when I'm eating unconsciously, the weight climbs quickly.

Before the accident, I found a nutritional supplement that was helping me stay healthy, naturally lose excess weight, and keep the pounds from creeping on, but after the accident, eating seemed to be the only pleasure left in life.

A friend had recently lost weight, so it made sense to ask her what she had done. I felt desperate to take the extra weight off, and I didn't think I could do it on my own, so I went to the weight loss clinic my friend referred me to for injections and a weight maintenance strategy.

They put me on a six-hundred-calorie diet. Obviously, it didn't matter what was in the expensive shots, I was going to lose weight on such a low-calorie eating plan! And I did.

Physically, I looked better than I had in years. On the outside, everything looked good. I was taking care of myself again as far as anyone else could tell. I was put together, and I showed up. I was putting on an award-winning performance that everyone was buying except for my family and my therapist.

All the activity was creating an illusion of strength, but being strong was destroying me, because I wasn't truly strong. It was all a front.

NOTES

1. J. K. Rowling, *Harry Potter and the Goblet of Fire* (New York: Scholastic, 2000), 695.

2. Haruki Murakami, *What I Talk About When I Talk About Running*, reprint edition (Louisville, KY: Vintage, 2009).

CHAPTER 8

Hope for the Future

I didn't know how to be happy, but I still believed that my Heavenly Father could help me.

I remember reading the shepherd David's words in 1 Samuel: "The Lord that delivered me out of the paw of the lion and out of the paw of the bear, he will deliver me out of the hand of this Philistine" (1 Samuel 17:37). This was the brand of my testimony. God had helped me before, maybe he could help me again.

When David defeated Goliath, it wasn't his first time using a sling. He wasn't just a shepherd and then suddenly the champion over Goliath. He had experiences that prepared him to fight Goliath. His faith had been deepened in God's protection before he attempted to defeat the giant. Not that the fight with Goliath was easy, but God had prepared him and strengthened David's faith before the challenge.

David's brothers were serving in the Israeli army while their younger brother David continued to tend the sheep at home. Their father Jesse sent David to bring supplies to his brothers in their war camp. When David arrived, he heard the ominous threats of the Philistine Goliath hurled toward the Israeli army. David didn't understand why someone didn't fight Goliath, so he approached King Saul and offered to fight the giant Philistine himself.

In a conversation with King Saul before David fought Goliath, "Saul said to David 'thou art not able to go against this Philistine to fight with him: for thou art but a youth and he a man of war from his youth' (1 Samuel 17:33).

"David said . . . 'The Lord that delivered me out of the paw of the lion and out of the paw of the bear, he will deliver me out of the hand of this Philistine'" (verse 37).

The lion and the bear had been his early Goliaths. The young shepherd witnessed how God had protected him from the lion and the bear, and this strengthened David's faith. Remembering God's protection gave David the courage and assurance that God would protect him again, even against the giant Goliath.

David's story reminded me again to consider God's goodness and God's past answers to my faith in Him. Because of my experience with previous losses, and because I could see how God had supported me before, I did maintain a sliver of hope that healing was possible. I didn't know how or when, but I knew it was possible.

When my second oldest daughter, Kristin, was only ten months old, she developed a high fever one night. The fever climbed swiftly. Her pale cheeks were flushed, and she quietly cried in discomfort. I did everything I could as a young mom to reduce her fever, including giving her baby Tylenol and putting her in a cold bath. After her late-night bath, she quieted down. Her cheeks were not as red and her fever not as fiery. I settled her into her crib, praying that she would get some rest and that I might get some rest too. I walked the short hallway from her room to mine, hoping she would be better when she woke in the morning. My then husband was traveling, and I was alone with just my three-year-old and my baby in our small home in Palm Harbor, Florida. I went to bed apprehensive and exhausted.

At 3:00 a.m., I heard Kristin awaken and start to wail. I quickly ran down the hall to her bedroom, but before I got to her, her cries suddenly stopped, and I heard the thump, thump, thump of her feet hitting the mattress. I knew she was having a seizure.

I knew it was a seizure, because a couple of months before, my friend Nancy had shared her memories of her oldest daughter having seizures when she was a toddler. Without the miracle of Nancy's story, I would have never known what was happening, and a startling situation would have been more frightening. With a little knowledge, the situation was scary but manageable. I called Nancy in the middle of the night to ask what to do, knowing I could reach her faster than a doctor at that hour. She reassured me that Kristin would be okay and that there wasn't much I could do during the seizure. Then Nancy said she was coming over. She arrived about ten minutes later to sit with my three-year-old, who was still sleeping in the third bedroom, while I took Kristin to the hospital.

My mother came with me to the hospital, and I welcomed her support. If Nancy hadn't come to the house, I would have had to awaken three-year-old old Stephanie to take her with us to the hospital, or my mom would have needed to stay with Stephanie, and I would have had to take Kristin alone. Thank goodness for a good, thoughtful friend.

We rushed to the emergency room, checked in at the front desk, and then sat in the waiting area to wait for someone to call us back to have Kristin checked. I hoped they would be able to give her something stronger that would bring her high fever down, but while we waited, she had another seizure. Frustrated, I marched to the front desk to let them know that my baby was suffering because they were delayed seeing her. I was certain once they examined her that they would have the means to help her.

Eventually, they did bring her back, and she was admitted to the hospital with a 105-degree temperature. She never had another seizure, but she remained quarantined in the children's ward for three days while they ran tests, identified the infection, and treated her.

The first morning in the hospital, our pediatrician visited. She is a good woman of faith that I had known as my own pediatrician from the time I was a young toddler. She said that the attendants had commented on how calm I was during the whole ordeal. Without me saying anything, she knew it was my faith in God that sustained me. I told her I knew that panicking would not have aided the situation. Then she said, "I don't know how people go through hard things who don't have faith in God." I agreed. There is a peace and strength that comes from knowing God is on your side.

In small and simple ways, my Heavenly Father sent blessings of preparation as he did in the weeks before Kristin had her seizure. I felt certain that hearing Nancy's story about her daughter's seizures was just what I needed and just what my Heavenly Father provided for me to prepare me for that experience. Hearing the doctor's affirming acknowledgment of the strength of faith in God further strengthened my faith. Always knowing that I could depend on him to prepare and help me makes all the difference.

I often hear 1 Corinthians 10:13 cited as suggesting that God will not give us more than we can bear. This verse speaks specifically to temptation. "But God *is* faithful, who will not suffer you to be tempted above that ye are able; but will with the temptation also make a way to escape, that ye may be able to bear it." I believe this scripture does imply that God will not tempt us above what we are capable of bearing, but there's a disclaimer also that suggests that he will not tempt us above what we can bear *with his help*. When I choose him, he provides the escape I need to bear it.

For me the answer is in Proverbs 3:5–6, where we're instructed to "Trust in the Lord with all thine heart; and lean not unto thine own understanding. In all thy ways acknowledge him, and he shall direct thy paths." It's not that I won't be called upon to bear heavy burdens, but that if I will put my trust in the Lord, not trying to figure it all out myself, and acknowledge his goodness, mercy, and power, *then* I can have faith that he will lead me and I can lean on his goodness and power.

These "rememberings" of God's righteousness and mercy helped me as I crawled out of the black abyss that I had been thrust into because of Carrie's and David's deaths.

I was, however, missing one important piece. My Heavenly Father loves me, as he does all his children. He sent his Son, our Savior, to die for our redemption. I understood that at some level, but not at a profound enough level that I could extend his divine love to how I felt about myself.

Despite the many times I had received impressions that David and Carrie were eternally safe and where they were supposed to be, and that the accident was part of God's plan for them, I persisted in blaming and berating myself for what had happened.

If the Spirit could inspire me to bring my arm in to protect me from permanent injury, and if God could arrange for the surgeon who knew the specific procedure James needed to prevent him from having a disabling injury to be at the hospital on a holiday when we arrived, surely that same God could have prevented the accident had it not been Carrie and David's time to move to the next realm of existence. On an intellectual level, I recognized the miracles, but I could not let it settle deep into my heart to help me heal.

While my therapist assisted me with EMDR and a safe place to discuss my pain, true healing could not take place until I learned to love and appreciate myself.

I knew that it wasn't okay to be unkind to others. Why then was it okay for me to be continuously unkind to myself? I said things to myself that I would never say to someone else. I know now that my Heavenly Father wants me to understand and internalize the vision he has of me. He wants me to know that I am his child and that I carry a divine spark from him.

I now understand "Thou shalt love thy neighbour as thyself" differently. "Jesus said unto him, Thou shalt love the Lord thy God with all thy heart, and with all thy soul, and with all thy mind. This is the first and great commandment. And the second is like unto it, Thou shalt love thy neighbour as thyself. On these two commandments hang all the law and the prophets" (Matthew 22:37–40).

Heavenly Father loves all his children, including me! He doesn't love me better or less than any of his other children. He loves purely, a concept that is hard to comprehend in our mortal state. He loves *me* purely. He and his son Jesus Christ love me with greater, purer love than anyone else can love me. Their capacity to love is beyond my grasp.

If I am to be like them, I will seek to love them and to love like they do. My mission is to seek to love everyone as they do, including to seek to understand God's love for me.

Charity is the pure love of Christ. When I'm invited to love my neighbor—meaning everyone—as I love myself, I'm invited to seek charity for *all*, including *myself*.

Charity is a gift from God. I cannot seek charity without God's help. Charity is impossible without God's help. He invites me to ask him to help me strengthen my love for him and my love for all his children.

My experience has been that as I learn to love and accept myself, my capacity to love and accept others expands exponentially. As I learn to be patient and kind with myself, my ability to be patient and kind with others also increases. It's a lesson I hope to continue to work on.

I have learned that my love and appreciation for myself and others starts with my thoughts. My thoughts create my emotions, which then influence my behavior.

The good news is I can choose my thoughts. My initial thoughts after the accident were, *This is horrible. How can I live with this? The pain is more than I can bear.* It felt terrible, but feeling terrible was appropriate for what I was experiencing. Grief is the necessary road to healing.

My thoughts kept me spinning in utter agony. *I'm a terrible person. I can't do anything right. All our pain is my fault. I don't deserve to live.*

As I continued to entertain these damaging ideas, I heaped additional suffering on myself. If I had continued thinking these thoughts much longer, I fear I wouldn't be here today writing this book, because these are the thoughts that lead to actions of self-destruction.

Thinking *There's something wrong with me because I can't be happy* was my undoing for a time. When I thought, *Maybe I can be happy in the future*, it gave me the space to adjust to my loss and created an opening for future possibilities.

One of the problems with grief is that there is no time line for how long it will last, but I learned there are things that can help healing, and things that can prolong grief.

In *Man's Search for Meaning*, Viktor Frankl shares his dehumanizing experience of being a prisoner in a concentration camp, an experience that I cannot comprehend. I can only imagine that it was far worse than my imagination can even conceive.

Frankl famously wrote, "Between stimulus and response there is a space. In that space is our power to choose our response. In our response lies our growth and our freedom."[1] I believe this is true.

What exists between stimulus and response are my thoughts and feelings. In my early pain, the space between stimulus and my response was miniscule, almost imperceptible. Over time, that space got larger, and with awareness, that space was much more noticeable. That gave me the space to choose.

I think we make a mistake when we consider Viktor Frankl's words. We may think that the response he refers to should look a certain way. In other words, that we should act like we're healed and all better and that it doesn't still hurt when we're not healed. But it does hurt.

That's the danger of his quote without context. If you read Viktor Frankl's book, you can see that he was still hurt. He still had to grieve what he lost. His experience was still extremely painful. *But* he didn't allow it to make him bitter. He didn't allow his captors' cruelty to make him cruel. He chose to be hurt, to grieve, and to recognize the pain and the cruelty. In it all, he chose to still be humane, to still exhibit love and compassion, and to still be a good person and to work toward healing.

I wonder if we make the mistake of thinking that our response to tragedy needs to be "I'm 100 percent great, and good, and everything is wonderful in my world." But denying our pain is not healing from, helpful to, or honoring our grief.

Our response after tragic stimulus could be deciding to grieve, deciding to learn about grief, and deciding to create time and space in our life for grief and healing and reviewing and adapting. That's when we create the growth and freedom Frankl wrote about. Because "when we are no longer able to change a situation, we are challenged to change ourselves."

Gradually, as I did the work of understanding my grief better, and as I practiced self-care, my thoughts changed to *I'll find a way to survive. I've been through horrible things before and things got better. Maybe this can too. Maybe I can be a whole again. Maybe I can feel happy again.*

After many months, my new, more encouraging thoughts became *I can be happy. I am happy. I am excited about life again. I love my kids, and I will hold onto that instead of the pain of losing them.*

The way we think about anything makes all the difference.

NOTE

1. Viktor Frankl, *Man's Search for Meaning* (Boston: Beacon Press, 2006).

CHAPTER 9

Emotional Triggers

*D*espite already dealing with heavy hardships, life continued to throw additional challenges our way. It felt unfair. We already had so much we were dealing with, why couldn't the world just stop and let us get off for a while?

I felt we should be exempt, like the kid with a pass from his doctor that says he doesn't need to participate in PE because of a physical ailment. I wanted a pass on life while I was slogging through trials. I wanted to present this pass to the universe, because my heart was broken.

Sometimes I wanted a pass on life for the remainder of my life, not just for a time. As if to tell the world, "This horrible thing has happened, so I'm opting out of engaging in life again." But that's not the way life works.

During my grief, the simplest demands were overwhelming. About six months after the accident, James was fully healed, and he was back to his tennis lessons at the neighborhood courts. One afternoon, I got a call from his tennis instructor that James had hit a car with his bike on his way to his lesson.

I felt heavy panic in my heart that was magnified by my recent horrifying experience. I was grateful to quickly learn that James was fine but rattled. We were relieved, but then we had to deal with the driver of the car, the insurance companies, and making decisions about how we were going to handle everything. The everyday challenges of life kept showing up to trigger me in addition to my grief.

After the tragedy of Carrie's and David's deaths, I experienced many emotional triggers. I learned the hard way that permission to grieve, patience in grief, and perseverance in healing are imperative. Healing my emotional triggers required all three. Without one or the other, my healing would be incomplete.

Triggers occurred when I felt set off by an object, an event, a place, or any other item in my environment that reminded me of what I'd lost.

After Carrie and David died, seeing David's empty bunk bed was painful. Driving past the neighborhood where Carrie's friend lived was heartbreaking. Seeing a movie that included a child dying was shocking and brought a flood of unpleasant memories. Being around other kids their ages, or watching parents interact with their kids, reminded me of the dreadful reality that I did not have my kids with me and I would not be able to raise them.

Two months after Carrie and David died, we attended a family reunion. For several years, from the time my oldest daughter was a baby, my mother's family gathered for a week at the beach on the east coast in St. Augustine, Florida, just a few miles from my mother's hometown of Palatka.

My mother is the oldest of eight living children, and I'm the oldest of thirty-three cousins. Each generation, my grandparent's posterity expanded exponentially. Therefore, each year the crowd expanded.

In the past, we loved these opportunities to reunite with our extended family, but our pain was fresh and raw that year. James was still on crutches, healing from his injuries. My physical injuries had mostly healed, but my spirit was broken.

This reunion was different also, because my cousin planned her wedding around the reunion while everyone was already in town. On one of the last days of the reunion, she got married on the beach where we were staying. A lot of the activity of the week had been helping my aunt and uncle prepare for the wedding.

A wedding arch was set up on the beach, with an ocean backdrop and seating for all the guests. Another uncle performed the ceremony as we all looked on under a cloudy sky and enjoyed a gentle breeze, the sound of crashing waves a short distance away, and sand beneath our feet.

After the ceremony, we walked the boardwalk back to the condos and prepared for an evening reception. A large rented event tent had been set up in the common area by the clubhouse between the buildings. It was a beautiful evening of music, dinner, and celebrating. I was happy for my cousin, but Ron and I couldn't help remembering that there would be no wedding for Carrie.

We would never watch Carrie grow up, fall in love, and marry the man of her dreams. After dinner, I noticed Ron had left and no one knew where he was. I left my table and went back to the condo to find him in our room. The wedding celebration was too much of a reminder of everything we had lost.

A few months later on the first Halloween night without Carrie and David, we walked the neighborhood with our friends and their kids. On Halloween night it had been a tradition to trick or treat with our friends. Just the year before, we had gathered for dinner and pictures at their house before making the rounds door to door. Of course, this year was different. Everything in our world was different. We were glad to be included but were incredibly sad since it was just James with us that year.

As we walked the neighborhood, the younger sisters of Carrie's and David's friend said what we were all thinking: "I miss Carrie and David." I could sense her mother's uneasiness at her comment, but she was just being honest. Kids have the ability to see and say the truth, an ability that we lose as we grow older and become more cautious.

On another occasion, I was driving a group of kids to a homeschool activity. As the kids loaded in my car, one of Carrie's friends asked if they would be safe and referred to the accident that Carrie died in. I was stunned. It was a punch to the gut, but I was reminded that he was just a child who did not understand the impact of his statement.

One day my daughter Stephanie came home livid because a friend's mother had talked to her about how Carrie and David had been unsafe because they weren't in car seats. The mom cited a study about the need for car seats for older kids. Of course, eventually this information would be universally known and accepted. Laws would be enacted to require car seats for children much longer than they were in 2007. Stephanie bristled at this mom's insensitivity in her suggestion.

Before Carrie's death, her good friend Lauren had moved from a few streets away to another neighborhood off the same main road but a couple of miles away. I have fond memories of dropping Carrie off to play, particularly one day when we were coming back from shopping.

Carrie had grown out of most of her clothes, and the spring weather prompted a shopping trip to a new little girls-only shop on the highway. As we shopped for her new clothes, Carrie repeatedly expressed her appreciation. We even found a pretty Easter dress for her to wear to church. She was particularly happy about a new T-shirt we purchased that said, "Mommy's Girl."

My heart filled with love for her sweet appreciation and her unabashed expression of love that she would wear on her new shirt. I wondered how many more months or years she would be willing to openly acknowledge her love for her mom and dad.

Carrie was my fifth child after all, so I had experienced the teenage years before. I knew how my teenagers wrestled with dependence versus independence. That perspective gave me a greater enjoyment of Carrie's innocence.

On the way home from shopping, we passed Lauren's neighborhood. Since we were close by, I suggested that Carrie call Lauren to see if she was available to play. Carrie was delighted when Lauren said she was available and invited Carrie to come over right then.

I turned the car around and drove Carrie to Lauren's house. I can still see the joy on Carrie's face when I dropped her off and watched her greet her friend. Playing with Lauren that day was a delightful, spontaneous event on a day of good things.

After the accident, driving past the store where we had shopped and driving past Lauren's neighborhood became a painful reminder again of all I had lost. I remembered Carrie's pleasure in finding new clothes to wear. I remembered her excitement to go play with a friend. I knew those experiences were in the past and I would never be able to share in her joy again here on the earth.

Each time I passed these places of shared memories, I was reminded of my loss. I would fall apart in anguished tears, knowing that Carrie was no longer here to spend time with or to thrill with shopping trips and unexpected visits with a friend.

I have since learned that these triggers are not outside of me. It feels as if they come from outside of me because they are an outside comment, visual, or reminder. But the outside stimulus created a reaction because of what was going on inside me.

I had thought that bringing up the painful past creates more pain, when what it does is bring the internal pain to the surface. People will often say they don't want to work on their grief because it will trigger memories. The choice isn't between feeling pain and not feeling pain. It's between facing our pain and not facing it. The pain exists either way. When I can face my pain, I can heal my pain.

Brené Brown suggests that hiding creates shame, and it's only in the exposure of our shame that we can overcome it. Of course, grief and shame are not the same emotions, but in my case, both were ever present. I had deep guilt and shame about my culpability in the accident.

Brené Brown distinguishes the difference between guilt and shame:

> Based on my research and the research of other shame researchers, I believe that there is a profound difference between shame and guilt. I believe that guilt is adaptive and helpful—it's holding something we've done or failed to do up against our values and feeling psychological discomfort.
>
> I define shame as the intensely painful feeling or experience of believing that we are flawed and therefore unworthy of love and belonging—something we've experienced, done, or failed to do makes us unworthy of connection.
>
> I don't believe shame is helpful or productive. In fact, I think shame is much more likely to be the source of destructive, hurtful behavior than the solution or cure.[1]

While guilt can be a useful tool to inspire change, misplaced guilt creates feelings of shame, which intensifies our pain and increases emotional triggers. Guilt implies an intention to harm, whether conscious or unconscious. There's a fine line between guilt toward change and guilt that keeps us ruminating and stuck. Misplaced guilt sent me into hiding. Hidden misplaced guilt is heavy and shame filled.

Brené Brown said, "Shame corrodes the very part of us that believes we are capable of change. If we can share our story with someone who responds with empathy and understanding, shame can't survive."[2] Thus, we need a compassionate witness to help us heal from our pain.

As I increasingly became more comfortable sharing my story, I felt the shame dissipate. For a long time, I would just say that the kids died in a car accident. When people asked more questions, I avoided the obvious, which was that I fell asleep at the wheel. I couldn't bear to admit it. I couldn't bear to imagine the judgment that was heaped on me for putting my children at risk by driving tired, especially since I have no recollection of being tired. I knew what people would think. I could not bear the guilt and shame of it all.

Over time, as I became emotionally stronger, I learned that it doesn't matter what other people think. I can own the truth, share my story, and allow others to think what they want to think.

Shame erodes our connections as well. Shame limits our ability to love and keeps us stuck in emotional triggers. As Brené Brown suggests, "shame can't survive" when we open up to others in vulnerable and meaningful ways. We need to love. We need a sense of belonging. Without love and belonging, our sense of self is damaged.

I've become acutely aware of how important connection is. It is a basic human need. In fact, Abraham Maslow's model of the hierarchy of human needs places love and connection just above our physical needs such as food, water, shelter, and safety. If our basic physical needs are not met, or if we don't feel safe, the attainment of those things become such a fierce focus that making a connection is beyond our capacity.[3]

I've learned that when bad things happen, it erodes our sense of safety, which can make connection difficult. When others reach out, it's hard for us to reciprocate, but allowing others in can help us rebuild our sense of safety. This is an ironic reality.

Again, Brené Brown:

A deep sense of love and belonging is an irreducible need of all people. We are biologically, cognitively, physically, and spiritually wired to love, to be loved, and to belong. When those needs are not met, we don't function as we were meant to. We break. We fall apart. We numb. We ache. We hurt others. We get sick.

When you get to a place where you understand that love and belonging, your worthiness, is a birthright and not something you have to earn, anything is possible.[4]

Unfortunately, what others say and do can be triggering, which causes challenges as we try to connect with people. In grief, my emotions were heightened. My ability to reason was reduced, which made it easier to misinterpret others' attempts to help.

In people's attempts to comfort grievers, they sometimes say things that aren't helpful. These comments can cause us to recoil. They minimize our pain with comments such as, "At least you have other children," or "At least you had eight years with him," or "God needed her more," or "He's in a better place."

Even though they are attempting to help and comfort with their comments, in response, our internal dialog often goes something like this: *Yes, I have other children that I love, but that does not take away the pain of losing my child. How ridiculous to think that I can dismiss my pain because I have other children.* Or, *Eight years is not long enough when I want him here with me forever. I feel cheated out of the time I might have had.* Or, *Who is this God who needs her more than I do? God has everything. Why does he need her?* Or, *He may be in a better place, but I can't think of a better place for him to be than right here with me.*

We wince at these well-meaning comments and feel a need to stand up for our pain and our suffering instead of feeling comforted. We want to respond with "how dare you!" instead of "thank you." I had to repeatedly remind myself of the intent of the comments rather than the exact words. When I remembered that they were sincerely wanting to help, this aided me in lessening the emotional trigger and appreciating their attempts to comfort. Of course, mostly people were kind and supportive, but as I practiced more useful thoughts about what others said and did, I found that my reaction to their offer of support was gratitude for their tremendous efforts. I knew it wasn't easy for anyone. A tragedy is uncomfortable, to say the least.

I learned that if I wanted people in my life, I must give them grace. As I've watched people's reactions to how others approach them after a loss, I've often wondered what friends and family have left that is safe to say. Recently, I saw a tirade on social media from a woman who was outraged by someone saying to her that they can't imagine what she's going through. Her complaint was that she was in a lot of pain, and they can't even take a minute to imagine what that's like for her. She had become so hypersensitive that there was hardly anything left that people could say to her.

The good news is that our response is always filtered through our thoughts. If I can find a better thought, I can experience a better reaction. "I can't imagine what you're going through," was one of the most frequent responses I heard. I get it! I couldn't imagine it either until I experienced it. The pain is unimaginable. It's an unthinkable pain you don't want people to experience. How can anyone understand the depth of devastating grief after the death of a child, much less two?

I'm grateful for the miraculous inspired thought and decision I made right after the accident that I would not be offended by anything anyone said. I would remember how uncomfortable it was for everyone and give them grace, remembering that the words they offered, no matter how unskilled, were offerings of love and comfort. No doubt the inspired instruction I received was a gift from God.

The challenge we face is that a tragic loss can create such strong emotions that it's a struggle to rise above the loss. Dr. Joe Dispenza explains that long-term memory is created by emotion. According to his research, the stronger our emotional tie to an event, the stronger the memory—good or bad. He teaches that when we have an emotional reaction, it creates chemistry in our body that causes physical sensations with each emotion. Some of these sensations are more prominent than others.

Dr. Dispenza also equates our subconscious with our body. Memories and beliefs are stored in our body as chemistry. When we recall the same memories over and over, we create this chemistry over and over, which creates what he calls a "state of being." We can literally become addicted to our emotional state. Because our subconscious can't tell the difference between our past, present, or future, when we invoke the emotion of a memory over and over, we are creating a state of being tied to our past.

When we experience a devastating loss, the memory is super charged, and if we don't get involved with our thinking and feeling process, we can easily fall into a state of despair, hopelessness, and victimhood. This was the dangerous precipice I was teetering on.

Dr. Joe Dispenza explains how this works:

As we begin to feel the way we are thinking . . . we begin to think the way we are feeling.

Thoughts are attached to mind, feelings connected to body. When mind and body are in unison, the end product: state of being.

After many years, we memorize a state of being, 'I am...[lazy, anxious, uncertain, short-tempered, dumb, etc].'

When feelings become the way we think, we can't think greater than we feel, we can't change. Because the body (feelings) control the mind (thoughts).

Change = thinking greater than how we feel.

When you see yourself as a victim, and have too much self-pity for too long, your body is conditioned to remember the feeling of suffering without much conscious thought. It feels normal/natural, it's who you are, and you find it hard to change.

Most people don't know that when they think about a highly charged emotional experience, the brain refires the exact same patterns, and they are firing/wiring their brains to the past.

We can relive the past over and over; this trains the body to remember that emotional state. When the body is the mind, that's a habit.[5]

In contrast, he advises, "To be empowered—to be free, to be unlimited, to be creative, to be genius, to be divine—that is who you are. . . . Once you feel this way, memorize this feeling; remember this feeling. This is who you really are . . ."[6]

Emotional triggers are caused by living in the past pain. These triggers brought me overwhelming distress and devastation. Some of this distress happened because I was feeling hijacked. I believed there was no cure for my pain since my circumstances could never change. Carrie and David were gone from this world, and nothing could reverse that reality.

In an article on thiswayup.org, they explained, "It is common for people to continue to have distressing thoughts, images, and feelings for some days, or even weeks, following the trauma. These reactions are common and are a sign that the body is recovering from a severe stress."[7]

My painful triggers, even my PTSD, were a signal that my mind was reliving the past and my body couldn't make the distinction between then and now. My mind was sorting it out. Over time, I came to understand that triggers aren't bad; they are just signals that there's more healing to do. I've learned the importance of accepting that healing takes time and effort.

For a time, I mistakenly believed the trigger was causing my pain, but the pain was within, and the trigger reminded me of my existing pain. The trigger pushed my pain button. As I let go of the pain of loss, the triggers dissipated. Again, giving myself permission to grieve, practicing patience as I grieved, and persevering through the pain of letting go and growing were vital to my healing. There are no quick fixes to grief.

On a Facebook grief group, a young woman shared that her mother loved butterflies. After her mother died, every time the daughter saw a butterfly, she would be reminded of her mom and she would say, "I love you, mom." This young woman had moved beyond the pain of her loss and remembered the love and happiness she shared with her mother.

I imagine this daughter may have first experienced a painful trigger when she saw butterflies after her mother's death since it reminded her of her mother and her pain, but over time, she let go of the pain and kept the love and gratitude.

I wanted to strengthen my love and appreciation for Carrie and David and move through my grief until I could let go of the pain. This is the model that helped me move from emotional triggers to freedom, love, and appreciation.

Mother's Day was destined to be a huge trigger for me as it is for many other women: those who have lost their mother or a child, those who want children but can't have them, those who have had miscarriages, those who are dissatisfied with motherhood, and those who are estranged from their children or are suffering from parental guilt. These and many other circumstances create pain for so many women during this holiday.

Not only had Carrie and David died, but it happened on Mother's Day as well. The very first Mother's Day without Carrie and David, a year after the accident, I was braced for the inevitable devastating pain. As It approached, I considered how I would manage. Would I go to church or would that be too heartbreaking? Will I survive the day and what will it look like?

The Friday night before Mother's Day Sunday, Ron and I went to dinner with another couple and left our teenagers, Dallin and James, at home to entertain themselves. After our evening with our friends, we drove home and entered the house through the back door. As we came through the door, we saw two backpacks on the floor in the kitchen. These were not ordinary backpacks; they were girl's backpacks.

We could hear the TV playing in the upstairs game room, and ex-pecting to find the boys entertaining two girls while we were gone, Ron bounded up the stairs to catch them with their unauthorized guests. It was not what he expected. Instead of finding teenage girls flirting with our boys, he discovered that our daughters, Stephanie, with her husband Chris, and Kristin, had flown home from college to surprise us.

What a beautiful surprise! What a wonderful, tender experience to have them come home so we could all be together on that very first an-niversary of when all our lives changed so drastically.

That Sunday I proudly went to church with my four loving children, imagining that our angels Carrie and David also sat with us on the pew. My heart was so full of love and appreciation for every one of our pre-cious children, and my whole feeling about Mother's Day forever shifted.

Instead of the unbearable pain, Mother's Day reminded me of all that I had—six beautiful children we loved that loved us. How blessed I am to be their mother. How blessed I am to be Carrie and David's mother. As I consider that if Carrie and David were only meant to be here on earth for ten and eight short years, it seemed I had two choices:

to not have been their mother or to have the joy of being their mother for their short time here and then forever in eternity.

I decided that even though the grief was hard, and the rebuilding of my crushed soul was gut wrenching, I would rather be their mother than not. To this day, I experience the pain of the memories for a time on Mother's Day weekend, but I also feel the overwhelming love and gratitude for my precious family.

Brené Brown wrote,

> Owning our story can be hard but not nearly as difficult as spending our lives running from it. Embracing our vulnerabilities is risky but not nearly as dangerous as giving up on love and belonging and joy—the experiences that make us the most vulnerable. Only when we are brave enough to explore the darkness will we discover the infinite power of our light.[8]

I've discovered that when I am willing to face my pain and my emotional triggers directly with effort, thought, and self-reflection, I can eventually find peace once again. And when I worked toward healing, I could hope to develop understanding.

As Dr. Joe Dispenza said, "A memory without the emotional charge is called wisdom." The emotional charge keeps our body, mind, and emotions in the past, but when we work through the emotional charge, we gain wisdom born of experience.[9]

NOTES

1. "Shame v. Guilt," brenebrown.com/blog/2013/01/14/shame-v-guilt/, January 14, 2013. Accessed June 2, 2020.

2. See "Guilt, Shame, and Vulnerability: 25 Quotes from Dr. Brené Brown," cathytaughinbaugh.com/guilt-shame-and-vulnerability-25-quotes-from-dr-brene-brown/. Accessed June 1, 2020.

3. See "Maslow's Hierarchy of Needs," simplypsychology.org/maslow.html. Accessed June 1, 2020.

4. See brainyquote.com/quotes/brene_brown_553094 and brainyquote.com/quotes/brene_brown_553067. Accessed June 1, 2020.

5. Joe Dispenza, *Breaking the Habit of Being Yourself,* reprint edition (Carlsbad, CA: Hay House, 2013).

6. Ibid.

7. See "I Feel Traumatised," thiswayup.org.au/how-do-you-feel/traumatised/. Accessed June 2, 2020.

8. See goodreads.com/quotes/357565-owning-our-story-can-be-hard-but-not-nearly-as. Accessed June 2, 2020.

9. Dispenza, *Breaking the Habit.*

Kristin and David, 2006

CHAPTER 10

Believing in Miracles

*There are only two ways to live your life. One
is as though nothing is a miracle. The other is
as though everything is a miracle.[1]*

—Albert Einstein

Before, during, and after the accident, I experienced many miracles.
Some were obvious to me, and I recognized them right away. Others were subtle, and I only noticed them when I looked back with new perspective.

Three years after the accident, the miracle came that I had longed for, worked for, and didn't fully believe would ever come, but nevertheless, I hoped for anyway.

In God's infinite wisdom, he allowed me to strive and fight before he gave me the biggest miracle of my life thus far. As I reflect on this miracle, I don't fully understand why I received such a blessing and so soon. I know I didn't deserve it, but through God's glorious grace, it came.

Two and half years after David's and Carrie's deaths, our congregation, called a ward, split. In our church, we are assigned to wards by geographic boundaries. You go to a specific ward because you live within those boundaries. When a ward grows and reaches a certain size, new boundaries are drawn, and the congregation is split into two wards.

The ward we lived in had grown and was split on the last Sunday of December 2009. A new bishop was called for our new congregation, and new leaders were called to serve with the new bishop.

The new bishop of our newly formed congregation asked my husband and me to meet with him. We agreed to meet, and my husband and I went to his small office just off the foyer in the church.

I was shocked when I arrived and he asked me to be the president of the Young Women organization, which is the teen girls group of our church, ages twelve through eighteen. Despite my expressed disbelief, I said yes.

If Carrie were still alive, she would have been twelve and in this group of girls I was being asked to lead. I would now be the leader of so many of her friends that I loved, but it was a painful reminder that Carrie wasn't there.

I left his office in a stunned daze, a state that by now I was somewhat used to. I could not believe I was going to be taking on this assignment. In the past, I had always accepted the volunteer responsibilities that I was asked to fill at church, and I felt compelled to continue to serve in any capacity I could.

As I stepped out of the bishop's office, I could hear a group of the girls practicing basketball in the gym just down the hallway. I wandered over to the gym door and peeked in, feeling the weight of my new duties. As I watched their enthusiastic play for a minute, I wondered how I was going to lead these beautiful girls. I had serious and understandable doubts about my capacity.

My eyes glazed over in confusion as I left the church and went home with all my doubts and fears.

When I agreed to the position, the bishop gave me a letter that said, in part,

> Julie, I want you to know that the Lord loves you and is aware of the challenges that you face. He is also aware of your need to progress and grow. If we were able to control the times and seasons of our growth opportunities, we might never reach our full potential. . . . I know this will be a heavy weight to carry but know that you do not carry it alone. I know that with God's help, all things are possible.

That next Sunday, my name was presented to the congregation as the new Young Women president. Later I heard that one of my daughter's friends leaned over to her mom and said, "Isn't that too hard?" She was right.

As the new president, I asked other women to be leaders also, filling the positions of counselors and secretary to the president and advisors to the girls' different age groups. I was incredibly blessed with willing and talented women who helped the program run smoothly.

Each week we met with the girls on Sunday and Wednesday nights. Sundays we provided gospel lessons. The girls were grouped into three age groups. Once a month we met as an entire group. The rest of the month they met with their smaller groups, and I met and helped with the lesson for the sixteen to eighteen-year-old girls.

On Wednesday evenings, we had activities: service projects, athletics, crafts, and other events.

I had filled this same position as the Young Women's president almost twenty years before in my congregation in Florida. The basic structure was similar, but in Florida, we had a smaller group of girls and leaders. I was young and inexperienced, and my challenge then was to believe that I should be in that position as a twenty-five-year-old mom of one baby, who felt like she had just graduated from high school.

In those twenty years between assignments as president, I had spent a lot of time with the teen girls in other positions, so I was very aware of the commitment I was making, but the added grief that I was carrying felt like too much.

The next month was spent organizing and getting to know the girls that I didn't already know. Being able to concentrate on creating structure offered some comfort and familiarity, but Sundays were particularly painful as I participated in Sunday lessons and watched these wonderful girls grow in their testimony of their Savior. The spiritual discussions often brought up the rawness of my feelings since my loss was still so fresh.

I was determined to make it work somehow. Few people knew how deeply I was struggling. On the outside, everything looked fine. I held it together and decided to "fake it until I could make it." That only worked for the first six weeks.

I believe in inspiration, and as February approached, I felt inspired that the theme for the annual New Beginnings program, a parent-daughter meeting, was to be motherhood.

These girls lived in a world that didn't celebrate motherhood, but I believe motherhood is a divine calling. I wanted the girls to look forward to marrying and having children no matter what other opportunities might also come their way. I also wanted them to gain a greater appreciation for their own mothers, an appreciation that may not be realized fully until they were mothers themselves. I felt impressed that God wanted that for them too.

With the leaders' and the girls' help, we planned our upcoming New Beginnings program around that theme. The girls were excited and even created a T-shirt design to celebrate the theme.

In the past, the New Beginnings programs had sometimes been big productions with lots of decorations, fancy desserts, and an involved evening program. I wanted to strip it down, to make it a lovely evening of appreciation that could be focused on the girls' mothers and the joys of motherhood.

We planned a simple evening of short presentations by the girls with a large bouquet of a couple of dozen roses as our décor. We met in one of the nicer but smaller rooms in the church and enjoyed a special evening of gratitude and anticipation for their bright futures.

As planned, at the end of the program, all the girls came to the front, picked a rose from the vase, and gave a rose to their mothers to show their love and appreciation—a beautiful ending to a beautiful program the girls had prepared for their parents.

I sat in stunned silence as I realized that I was the only woman in the room who did not receive a rose. Even the other adult leaders had daughters in the room. I'm not sure why I hadn't expected or realized this would be the case. Without Carrie there, I did not receive a rose from my daughter.

After a long and exhausting day of preparation and disappointment, my tears were close to the surface. Everyone moved to the recreation room for dessert.

I was alone. I watched the small gatherings of parents and daughters. A few parents broke away to greet me and thank me for the program. All I could focus on was the deep pain I felt at not having my daughter there with me.

That was the beginning of a new spin into darkness. I spiraled downward into the depths of despair. I continued to show up each week, pretending that all was well, but a couple of the leaders around me knew that things weren't what they seemed.

One day on the phone with one of my counselors, I poured my hurting heart out to her. I cried, "I just want to sit on the back row. I don't want to be leading any more. I want to disappear into the background."

She replied, "That is not who you are." Maybe not, but that was who I had become.

Each anguished week my despair and my depression grew. I called my bishop weekly asking to step down. He always replied that he couldn't let me do that. He felt certain that the Lord was trying to bless me with this assignment, but all I could see and feel was the pain.

One day, I met with my bishop in his office. Again, I tearfully expressed my challenges. He suggested that if I had more faith, I would be able to bear my burden. In exasperation I said, "If I didn't have faith, I wouldn't be here!" I often felt that he didn't appreciate the pain and challenge of grief, but I wouldn't wish this pain on anyone.

Of course, I could have just refused to do it, but it wasn't in my nature. In fact, it was unusual for me to be so vocal about my difficulties. In past assignments, I had borne my struggles with solitary patience, rarely reaching up for support from the bishop. I was opposed to showing what I saw as weakness.

This was different. It wasn't just weakness; it was utter desperation. I was falling into a deep, dark hole and grasping for anyone or anything that could help me.

I could not escape my skin. I could not escape my misery. I imagined getting into my car and driving as far as I could go to flee from my hopeless life and my terrifying thoughts. I tried to work out the details of my escape in my mind, but I knew it wouldn't work. Wherever I went, I would still be there.

The pain was too great and exhausting. I was depleted. I had nothing left. I feared ending my life was the only answer, except that I was still rational enough to realize the devastation I would leave behind. Having lived through my brother's death by suicide, I understood all too well what that would mean for my family, and I couldn't do it.

I continued to go to therapy. I had seen Mary for two years, and she became increasingly concerned about my wellbeing. Her concern was so great that she called me at home to check on me, which was not her usual practice. She always recommended that her clients rely on other support systems between appointments.

Eventually, she suggested medication. In the two years we had worked together, she knew me well enough to see the dangerous shift and the warning signs.

She had never suggested medication before. She preferred that her clients work through their difficulties instead of relying on drugs to mask their emotions. At this point, she was concerned that the trauma I had experienced had created such a shift in my brain that the chemistry had changed, and I might not be able to find my way out without the aid of prescription medications.

Mary urged me to go to my doctor right away and ask for antidepressants. I thought this might be the answer too. I knew I was crashing, and I worried that I might not make it back this time. I made an appointment and met with my doctor. He prescribed medication for me, which I picked up and started right away.

Two days later, I started hallucinating and hearing voices in my head. I immediately called Mary. She asked what I was taking and how much. When I told her, she was shocked and upset at the dosage and suggested that I should have been on a quarter of that dose.

I don't like prescription drugs anyway, and this experience scared me so bad that I put the anti-depressants in my drawer and never took them again.

Once again, I was left with no answers, only excruciating pain that I felt unable to manage. I started to be more vocal about my pain hoping that someone would have an answer.

My frequent frantic calls to my bishop continued. I told him I could no longer do the job he wanted me to do. His answer was to strengthen the organization with others that could carry the load. This made no sense to me. If they were carrying the load, why was I still in the position? But he insisted.

Mother's Day, which was also the anniversary of the accident, was fast approaching. The closer I got to May, the further I fell into darkness. One day a neighbor friend Linda, who my bishop had put in charge of my duties while I was out "sick," texted to ask how I was doing. It was midday, and I was still in bed. I answered "fine," but Linda persisted and said she was on her way over.

A few minutes later, Linda was at my door, and I answered in my robe. I invited her in, and she followed me into the family room. I sat on the couch across from her, unable to meet her gaze as she reassured me and shared a message that she felt compelled to share.

She drew a large rectangle and said that each of us has a certain level of capacity. Certain trials or tasks come along that challenge our capacity. She suggested that my capacity was being filled with my trials, which is why I felt so inadequate in the moment. I had little capacity left for anything outside of dealing with my grief.

Even in my state of confusion, what Linda explained made some sense, and it's a model that I share with people still today. But it didn't explain how to move beyond the pain of deep grief.

I was still beating myself up, because I didn't know how to be okay, much less happy. I was miserable and making everyone around me miserable, which encouraged me to stay isolated as much as possible.

In April we had a weekend campout and hike for the Young Women. I was still trying to muddle through with my duties however ineffective I felt. I asked my husband to come pull the trailer and help with set up. He agreed.

My problems consumed my mind always. When I ran into a friend at the campout and we had a moment to talk away from everyone else, I talked about my problems and how depressed I was. I recognized that my problems had become so overwhelming that it was all I could think about or talk about.

It was a vicious pattern of constantly talking about my problems. I felt bad that it was all I talked about. Then I would isolate because I didn't want to be endlessly talking about my problems. The despondency continued.

During the hike that weekend, I walked with our ward's camp director. As we fell in place behind the girls, I once again opened up about my relentless struggles. I told her, "I feel like God is punishing me."

She stopped and looked at me. "Everything God does, he does to bless us," she stated. Her words went straight to my heart, and I knew she spoke the truth.

The darkness continued to consume my soul over the next couple of weeks, but as I reflected on God's blessings and altered my thinking to *Maybe God isn't punishing me, maybe he's trying to bless me*, the possibility ignited a spark within me.

The Sunday before Mother's Day, the bishop arranged to give me a special priesthood blessing after our church services. As mentioned in Mark 16:18, "They shall lay hands on the sick, and they shall recover."

As I sat in Sunday services beforehand, I could not focus at all. My heart was devoured in darkness and confusion. I could emotionally and physically feel this tangible darkness within me. After the meeting, I walked despondently to the bishop's office. I was lifeless.

My bishop and my husband placed their hands upon my head as the bishop declared a blessing upon me in the name of Jesus Christ. I don't remember any of the words he said, but through the power of the priesthood, he infused me with the Spirit of God and all darkness fled. The darkness that had consumed my heart and soul that I could see and feel only an hour before was gone.

Within hours, I felt healed from the pain that had gripped my soul for months and years. I felt as if God had turned the light on. I had walked into that office lifeless, damaged, and despairing, and I walked out with hope and love. That is the power of God.

The painful assignment to lead my daughter's friends had indeed been a catalyst to my healing. The difference was palpable. Other people had picked up my slack, but I began to cover my own assignments willingly and gratefully.

Pure joy and real purpose reentered my life. I went to the next campout with enthusiasm. I interacted with the girls, conducted meetings, and joined in the activities.

When my daughter Kristin married her boyfriend, Joel, later that year, Stephanie said, "You weren't this happy when I got married."

She was right. Stephanie got married only seven months after the accident. My world had been destroyed, and I was functioning from the rubble, but when Kristin got married, I had found joy again through the power of God.

My healing was sudden and miraculous, and I could not deny God's power that made it possible. I have often reflected on why Heavenly Father chose to heal me in such a dramatic way. I have felt unworthy of his blessing, and I have mourned with my friends who have not had this same remarkable change of heart. Only recently have I been inspired to understand that my Heavenly Father sent this blessing so I could testify of his power to heal. He truly wants to heal all, but we must choose to engage in our own healing. Even if healing doesn't come suddenly, healing is available to everyone.

Recently, I heard Russell M. Nelson, world-renowned heart surgeon and president of The Church of Jesus Christ of Latter-day Saints, say to a child, "The Lord loves effort, because effort brings rewards that can't come without it."

I acknowledge the tremendous blessing that God sent me. The blessing is undeniable and powerful. I also see that I put forth effort toward my healing. I could not have done it without God, but I believe that my effort put me in a position to receive his gift.

I felt whole and complete, but God had even more healing ahead for me.

———

NOTE

1. Albert Einstein; see goodreads.com/quotes/987-there-are-only-two-ways-to-live-your-life-one. Accessed June 2, 2020.

CHAPTER 11

Spiritual Practice

*Every good gift and every perfect gift is from above
and cometh down from the Father of lights.*

—James 1:17

*E*very bit of healing, every bit of hope, every bit of progress and light in my life came from one decision—to continue to believe in God and his goodness, despite my pains, griefs, and traumas.

I never doubted that God existed. I only doubted my ability to access his glory and power. I doubted my ability to do what needed to be done to live in purpose and joy.

I understand now more than ever how grief affects our souls. It sends us into darkness and confusion, but it is meant to be a part of the healing process. When I began to fight against my grief, that was when I got into trouble.

The Sunday after the accident, I went to church. Ron and my family suggested that it might be too hard, that I was justified in staying home, and I knew they were right, but I felt compelled to go. I yearned for something familiar and for the spiritual refresher that I so desperately needed and which I had felt before when I attended Sunday services.

We arrived and sat in the back just as the service began and snuck out the back just as quickly when the service ended. I wanted to be there, but I didn't want to engage with people.

A visiting speaker told about his experience as a land developer. He explained how as he would walk the job sites he would overhear the workers complaining about certain design decisions. He noticed that without the full picture and an understanding of what they were trying to accomplish and why certain things needed to be the way they were prepared, the laborers didn't appreciate the plans.

As he overheard each complaint, he understood the reason it was planned the way it was, even if they didn't with their limited knowledge of the scope of the project. He equated it to us as we live our lives questioning God's wisdom in allowing certain things to happen to us.

We often plead with our Father in Heaven: "Why does it have to be so hard?" Without the developers plans, we can't understand why life progresses the way it does. But God, the master developer, in his wisdom, knows the beginning from the end, and he designs our experiences exactly as we need them for our growth and learning.

As I listened, I knew his message was for me. I knew I was right in the middle of such an experience. I didn't fully understand why my family was asked to experience such immense pain, but God was in charge. If I humbly submitted to his will, it would all be for my good and for the glory of God. In theory that seemed like a glorious idea, but in practice, it proved to be almost impossible to keep that perspective.

I had never met the speaker and didn't see him again for two years. Two years later, I shared with him how powerful his message was that Sunday so many months before. He told me that he had not known of our loss before he spoke and that he learned about it afterward.

Once again, God had provided a miracle and inspired a speaker who did not know me to share exactly what I needed to hear. I've reflected on that message many times over the years.

I've also reflected on the miraculous blessing of being there that Sunday to hear God's message for me. That first Sunday after our tragedy confirmed my conviction to always try to be at the right place at the right time.

When my friend suggested that God only blesses us, and that truth resonated with my heart, I learned a little more about the nature of God. I understood at a different level my Heavenly Father's desire to bless us.

As Jesus taught, "Blessed are those that mourn: for they shall be comforted." That comfort that is offered is more than just our friends and family that show up at a funeral or who bring a meal or mow our lawn during tough times. It is the comfort and "peace of God, which passeth all understanding." This comfort will guard "your hearts and minds through Christ Jesus."

It is my belief that each friend who offers help, each family member who attempts to ease our burden—each and every moment is blessed by God and his angels.

Even in pain and suffering, he is blessing us. Even when we can't feel it—or maybe especially when we can't feel it—he is blessing us. He continually offers us experiences in which to learn and grow if we are willing to live in faith.

Faith doesn't mean we have all the answers. Why do we think it does? If I don't know how to live with my pain, does that mean I don't have faith? I don't think so.

"Faith is the substance of things hoped for, the evidence of things not seen" (Hebrews 1:11). As one religious leader suggested, "Hope comes of faith, for without faith, there is no hope. In like manner, faith comes of hope, for faith is 'the substance of things hoped for.' "[1]

Hope is essential. In some divine manner, faith, hope, and charity are intermingled in an eternal expression of God in our lives and never is this more evident than when we are suffering the pain of loss.

We are warned not to doubt. In Matthew 14:28, Jesus walks out to his disciples on the sea. When Peter sees him on the water, he asks, "Lord, if it be thou, bid me come unto thee on the water." And Jesus answers, "Come."

Peter steps out onto the water and walks toward Jesus, but he is troubled by the boisterous wind and the waves and begins to sink. He cries out, "Lord, save me."

"And immediately Jesus stretched forth his hand." Immediately! And then he asks, "O thou of little faith, wherefore didst thou doubt?" (verse 31).

In these short seven verses, Matthew 14:25–31, we are taught about the power of faith and the weakness of doubt. As Peter kept his attention on Jesus, he was successful on drawing on the powers of heaven to do what seemed impossible—to walk on water. But as his attention was drawn to the wind and the waves, he doubted and began to sink.

That first Sunday at church, with an inspired speaker who delivered God's message, Jesus immediately stretched forth his hand to keep me from sinking into despair. Repeatedly he immediately stretched forth his hand to save me as I walked through the refiner's fire.

In my own journey across the impossible waters of grief, I can see where I looked away from the Savior and focused on the noise of my challenges. It was all for my good. I had to experience the stark difference between faith and doubt. It was a meaningful lesson that I draw on every day and am still learning. And that's as it should be.

It's okay that I don't have everything figured out. It's okay that my faith isn't perfect. It's okay if I still find myself floundering in doubt too often. Nothing has gone wrong.

To God, I am like a child. I am learning. We don't berate a child for not already knowing all the lessons of life. But we do mistakenly think that once we are eighteen, graduated from high school, college age, married, or parents, we should suddenly know everything and should have perfect faith and all the answers. In that way, we are no better than an impatient know-it-all teenager.

Just as I shouldn't expect my children to know everything, God doesn't expect me to know everything either. He continues to lead me and teach me. It is when I'm proud and when I don't understand my lack that I get into trouble and stop learning the lessons God has for me.

We send our children to school to grow and learn, and God sends us to earth to learn the lessons in the school of life. The school of life is tough, but we make it harder when we think we should be getting straight A's without even going to class.

Having never experienced the pain of the loss of two children and having never experienced the pain of guilt of being the driver of the car, how could I expect to know how to navigate such a journey? I couldn't!

It was impossible, but not with God. With God, all things are possible. I just had to keep searching and finding my way with his omnipotent help.

Truly, one of the challenges of grief is how difficult it becomes to feel the Spirit of God when we're in tremendous pain. Our emotions and senses are overcome with our pain, making it nearly impossible to feel our Heavenly Father's love and support.

The footprints in the sand poem has become cliché, but the message is clear and eternally true: When we can't even comprehend, God and his heavenly and earthly angels are near, holding us in their arms and carrying us through.

When I went back to my therapist Mary after my miraculous healing experience and explained how I had been healed through the power of Christ, she was not surprised.

She said she had felt a tremendous conviction that healing would come, but she didn't know how or when. I think that's the same for all of us in all our challenges. With God's help, we can be healed, even though we don't always know how or when.

However, we must choose. In the story of Mary and Martha, Martha complained to Jesus that Mary wasn't helping with the dinner preparations. Instead, Mary sat at Jesus's feet to be taught. And Jesus said, "But one thing is needful: and Mary hath chosen that good part, which shall not be taken away from her."

I had to choose "that good part." It's against the laws of heaven for God to give us a blessing that we don't desire. Everything begins with desire. "I the Lord search the heart . . . even to give every man according to his ways and according to the fruit of his doings." God searches our heart and gives the gifts we desire.

As spiritual leader Neal Maxwell advised, "It is up to us. God will facilitate, but he will not force. Righteous desires need to be relentless."[2]

In my mind's eye, I see angels round about us, ready to bless us according to our desires and God's will. I believe God has so much more for us than we can even imagine. I've had a taste of it, and I desire more. But as the angels wait, they cannot act against our will.

They wait, and wish, and hope that our desire will be to receive the blessings of heaven. And as we desire, they move toward us and bless our lives. As we reject the blessings of heaven, our angels stand at a distance and weep for what they have to give but are unable to share.

Now I understand even more acutely that it's even more important to hold on to spiritual practices despite how we feel. Because pain can numb our senses, holding onto faith and hope can be a challenge. My spiritual practices looked different after the impact of tragedy, but a simple, imperfect spiritual practice had tremendous impact in my life.

When I was a young mom living in Florida, I was asked by my bishop to teach an early morning daily scripture study class for the high schoolers in our congregation before they started their school day.

One night at a training meeting, I witnessed the speaker pick up his scriptures and testify of the power of the book—not just the words, but the book itself. "When you hold the scriptures, you can feel the power in them," he said.

I believed his testimony of the scriptures, and his words have remained with me as a reminder of their importance. I gained a greater understanding of the sheer power of just their presence, in addition to the power of the words contained to transform my life for good. We would never think of not feeding our body. We are educated to feed our intellect, but do we recognize the literal necessity of feeding our soul?

I remember how much the Gideon pocket-sized New Testaments with Psalms and Proverbs meant to me when I was a young child. I don't remember how I got one, but I believe they were distributed at school. Of course, my mom made sure we had scriptures at home, but I loved the light-weight pages and the tiny, inspiring words of the small books.

After the accident, and because of my injuries, I had difficulty picking up my full-sized scriptures when I got home, but I had a small, pocket-sized version that my mother had recently given me for Christmas that was stored in a drawer in my nightstand. This small book reminded of my love for those small Bibles from elementary school.

In my darkest hours when I was unable to focus on reading, I remembered the man's testimony that there is power in the book. I held this small book of scripture to my chest to feel that power and the promises contained in them.

It was like a meditation to lie there with the book. Often, I attempted to read the verses, but my concentration was nonexistent. Trying to understand what I read was a futile effort; however, as I continued to try, my daily interactions with scriptures definitely changed.

I believed in the power of the book to help me heal even if I understood the words or not, so I persisted in holding the book and reading in short spurts.

My prayers changed from the routine morning and evening petitions offered as I knelt by my bed before the accident, to all-day simple and desperate pleadings for comfort and understanding after the accident.

Dear God, how can I go on? Over the months and years, God heard me and answered my prayers with glimpses of hope and faith as I was prepared to hear and learn.

My daily and weekly spiritual practices included holding my scriptures, offering continuous prayerful pleadings, and showing up at church.

My inadequacies were ever present, and it would have been easy to abandon all my spiritual practices completely. I'm grateful that with Heavenly Father's guidance, I not only persisted, but I also allowed modifications that suited my new circumstances.

Today I love diving deeply into the scriptures, but my simple practice of holding the book and feeling its power during a time of duress was exactly what I needed.

Now I can focus on my spiritual growth in regular meaningful ways. I love to seek answers to my questions in the scriptures, with my journal by my side. Writing the impressions and thoughts I have while I study deepens my understanding and keeps me focused on what I'm learning. This pondering of the divine is a form of meditation for me. I'm continuously discovering more and more about the power of meditation and deep pondering to enhance my scripture study and prayer. I always want to enhance my ability to listen.

I am intentional about my spiritual growth, desiring more and more understanding and Godly strength and power. I know the power of God. I have felt his miraculous power. I intimately know his power to save and redeem.

I also know that my knowledge of his omnipotence is limited. Knowing what I do know, I desire to know more, to access his glory and power in whatever way he inspires me to do so. I would not skip a day of meals. Why would I skip a day of feeding my spirit? And yet, sometimes I do. It is the great irony to know from where my blessings come and to not partake always. Evidence of my weakness.

I'm reminded of the painting of Jesus standing at the door knocking. The door is conspicuously missing a doorknob. The painting reminds me that Jesus has no access unless I choose to open my heart to his love and healing.

I have often felt that I am in a tug of war with earth and heaven. I live between mortality and the eternities, having those I love on both sides of existence.

Carrie and David connect me to heaven in a powerful way. Because of their deaths, I have studied death and dying in addition to grief and healing. I have felt the realities of our post-mortal lives. I have born the burden of learning to love my life here while longing for my life there.

I believe we will always feel as though something is missing until we return to our eternal home. I also believe that God intends us to live with purpose and joy while we are here. He has given us the gift of life and a powerful desire to live, despite the pains we endure.

I'm grateful for my connection to the eternities and for the reality of Carrie and David's continued existence in heaven and in my heart.

NOTES

1. Dieter F. Uchtdorf, "The Infinite Power of Hope," *Ensign*, Nov. 2008.

2. Neal A. Maxwell, "According to the Desire of [Our] Hearts," *Ensign*, Nov. 1996.

David and James, Grand Canyon, 2005

CHAPTER 12

Grief Myths

---

*Sometimes the smallest things take
up the most room in your heart.*[1]

—Winnie the Pooh

*A*s I finish my work on this book, our world is in commotion because of the coronavirus pandemic. When you read this, it may have passed, but I doubt its effects will leave our world the same. The same week that we started to feel the tremendous effects of the pandemic, I moved.

At the same time the world was changing, my husband and I sold our home, moved into a temporary apartment, and put the rest of our things in storage. As a community, the familiar was ripped from us from small to big ways—from the threat of sickness and death to the simple ability to go out in public, eat dinner out with friends, or send our kids to school.

When we sold our house, we moved away from our familiar surroundings while the world changed dramatically. I no longer had access to my piano or my art supplies, which all went to storage. Events were canceled, travel was canceled, and our businesses were gravely affected. I was knocked off balance.

I recognized that I was experiencing loss and grief. I knew from my experience with grief that I would do myself a disservice if I didn't acknowledge my losses and my pain. I made a list of all I had lost in just two weeks.

I listed the canceled family gatherings, the financial losses, the canceled show, the closed theaters and restaurants, my stored piano, the lack of space, the inability to shop online, the limited supply of toilet paper, the postponed trips, and more. I listed it all. It was a long list.

I understand that focusing on the positive and what I'm grateful for isn't enough. My grief would remain hidden and hurtful if I didn't acknowledge it.

We associate grief with death. Sometimes we associate grief with divorce or a diagnosis. But all too often, we don't recognize the dozens of losses that can create feelings of grief.

Some griefs are small, and other griefs are life altering. We know what has affected us in small ways and what has affected us in large ways. Comparing our own grief is instructive. Comparing our grief with another's grief is destructive.

Too often we discount our pain with statements such as, "At least I don't have it as bad as . . ." or "I should just be grateful for what I do have." Discounting our grief does not help us resolve it. Grief is meant to be a season, not a lifestyle.

Just a few weeks after Carrie and David died, I visited my friend Lynn who had been diagnosed with cancer a few months before. She was homebound and on oxygen. I also knew that she had lost two babies, among other challenges. She expressed her sorrow at my loss, and I responded, "My challenges are not as great as yours."

She immediately stopped me. "It is not worthwhile to compare," she stated. "You have experienced a great loss. Don't discount that."

Just before the funeral, Lynn sent me a card of sympathy, within which she listed some things to consider as we planned for the kids' burial. Having buried two babies, she had a list of specific things to think about, one of which was to do what we felt comfortable with regardless of what others suggest. I appreciated her loving encouragement.

We have been trained to appreciate the intellect. Our schools are set up to inspire intellectual learning, as they should be. From a young age, we are praised for our educational accomplishments, and thus we are conditioned to appreciate academic prowess. We may be trained in spiritual matters, such as me being taught to go to church and develop spiritual practices. Unfortunately, we are off balance in emotional training. We even lack a vocabulary for it. Thank goodness for children's literature, which at least introduces the idea of emotions.

A perfect example is the Winnie the Pooh stories by A. A. Milne. The Winnie the Pooh characters exhibit basic emotions and states of being, such as sadness, joy, appreciation, acceptance, enthusiasm, fear, anxiety, empathy, and sincerity. They are stories of emotions and how we deal with them.

Adult literature also exhibits emotional stories. We see how the character's actions are influenced by his or her emotions, and yet too often we are devoid of emotional expression in our lives, except those few emotions we deem as positive and thus worthwhile. We feel the emotions, but we judge them and therefore pick and choose which emotions to show. Unfortunately, when we suppress our "negative" emotions, we simultaneously suppress our "positive" emotions. We say we want to be happy, but we don't understand how our happiness is affected by our inability to feel sadness.

I learned that our emotions need and deserve the light of day. They need attention and air just like our intellectual and spiritual pursuits. As a society, we are focused on action and achievement. Because we live in a world wondering what we've done lately, creating the space for healing can be extremely difficult. Sometimes we take the time to celebrate the exciting moments, but we do not take enough time to experience the painful occasions. We go to the funeral and expect closure.

Our physical experience is an instructive model for our emotional experience. In college, I broke my foot running barefoot up a flight of concrete stairs at the apartment complex. The pain stopped me immediately. I felt the pain and responded to it. My roommates borrowed a friend's car and drove me to the health center on campus. The x-rays confirmed that my foot was broken, and they casted it and my leg to keep it protected and stable. Over the next few weeks, I was advised to limit my movement and take special precautions to promote healing.

But in my painful emotional experiences, I felt compelled to act strong for my family and my friends. At least I understood in the beginning the need to be still and protect my heart to work through the pain. But when I became inpatient and hit that imaginary deadline for suffering, I began to pretend I was okay. I began to figuratively walk on the pain and ignore the affects and act strong.

Our pain requires space. My heart aches for mothers who have lost children and feel compelled to go back to work just days after their child has died. I did not have that experience, but I know many who have.

During my divorce when my children were young, I would come home from work, put on my exercise clothes, and after feeding my children and putting them to bed, I would exercise to recordings in my front room. Afterward, I would often turn on sad music and lay on the floor between the speakers and cry.

I thought I was pathetic at the time, but looking back and knowing what I know now, I was doing exactly what I needed to do. I was allowing space for my grief. I was expressing my grief and allowing it to move through me both in physical activity and in tears. Emotions are energy in motion. They need and want to keep moving.

Now I am extremely sensitive to grief and its impact. I know the heavy burden the griever carries. I also have tremendous hope for the griever and their healing. I know that with proper care, their experience can bring what researchers are now calling post-traumatic growth. This hope and knowledge allows me to work with grievers without being affected by their pain.

A few years ago, I was in an association meeting of professionals. A speaker from a local charity had come to our gathering to discuss a service project we were considering doing with her organization. As she spoke stoically about the recent devastating loss of her husband, which was the reason the charity was established, I felt her anguish.

It hit me with tremendous force, and I realized that I was going to break down in this meeting with my peers. I decided to stop resisting the flow of tears and I allowed it to happen. At the time, I thought I was feeling a residual sadness of my own grief and the loss of my children. Later, I understood that I had taken on her pain and expressed it in a way she had been unable or unwilling to.

I hope that by sharing and expressing her pain I was able to relieve her suffering in some small way. I'm sure I will never know, but that is my intention. I know that we are much more connected to each other than we realize.

As the pandemic spread across the world, I felt as if an avalanche had fallen on me and engulfed me. As I worked through my experience, I called a friend that I knew could support me in more understanding. As we spoke, I recognized that I was not only feeling my own grief but also the grief of society for all that we had lost and were losing.

Unfortunately, I was absorbing the grief and not releasing it. I chipped away at the avalanche, choosing to transform the pain I was feeling into light and love. Little by little, I felt the energy leave my body in blowing winds of white sparkling dust. Again, I was grateful for the miracle of greater understanding.

In this experience, I had a visual. I saw grievers as being crushed by a boulder of pain. The boulder was too large and heavy to just push aside. In order to lift the boulder, they needed to chip away at it, and they needed to be able to view it as not one big boulder but as small rocks that combined to make a large, imposing stone.

When we view it as one unit, we can't see the possibility of moving it, but when we see it as small pebbles or sand to be chipped away at, it's much more doable and approachable.

Then I thought about the act of chipping away. To be more efficient in chipping away, it made sense that building strength would be an advantage. Each act of chipping away built strength for the next strike of the pickax. Inspiring input is another way to add strength to our efforts. Inviting others—family, friends, professionals, and God—to support us in chipping away and building strength increased our effectiveness.

As I listened to sad music and cried at night after my divorce, I was chipping away and removing a pebble each evening until the pain dissipated. As I met with my therapist after the accident, I was seeking support, chipping away, removing rocks, and gaining strength to remove more. When I exercised or played tennis, I was chipping away and gaining strength. When I hired a life coach, I was welcoming support, chipping away, and gaining strength. When I focused on increasing my spiritual strength and kept my eyes on Jesus, I was inviting support, chipping away, and gaining strength.

I couldn't see it at the time, and I didn't feel the effects of my efforts right away, but all the little things I did to deal with my pain and to strengthen myself helped me to remove the boulder of grief and pain. All this activity required a hunger for change, a hope that it was possible, and an understanding of how.

As Henry Ford said, "Whether you think you can, or you think you can't—you're right."[2] In other words, if you think you can, you will. If you think you can't, you won't.

We often hear that we will carry our grief forever. This is never truer than for the mother who has lost a child. She is told that she will grieve her loss for the rest of her days. I don't believe that's true. I don't carry my grief every day. In fact, I experience occasional sadness, but I do not grieve my losses continuously. If you believe you can move through the grief and live with joy again, you will. If you believe you can't, you won't, because you won't try, you won't seek help, and you won't recognize the opportunities for healing.

When the fallacy that we must heavily grieve the rest of our life after the death of a loved one is perpetuated, it causes great harm. First, it breaks down the desire to try to move forward through grief. Instead, we think, *if this is my fate I might as well get used to the pain.* Second, if you do start to move through the pain, you start believing that you must not have loved them enough.

The thought *I must grieve in order to prove my love* is particularly damaging. Did you love them before they died? Of course, you did! You loved them deeply before the pain of grief. Grief is not necessary to love. In fact, greater love and gratitude is experienced once we release the grief, but the expectation that you will grieve forever can stand in the way of moving beyond the pain of loss.

There are many choices in grief. I choose to believe we can heal from grief. I choose to believe that I can love deeply and release the pain of loss. I choose to believe that people do not die before their time. I choose to believe that Carrie and David are encouraging my family and me from their eternal vantage point. I choose to believe that they had accomplished what they needed to accomplish here and were called home to their Heavenly Father. I choose to believe that God knows better than I do what is for our greater good. I choose to believe that I am blessed to be Carrie and David's mother despite the pain that blessing has caused me. These choices were hard won. They did not come in an instant. I fought hard to gain these convictions, and I choose to continue to affirm these truths.

Commonly, we refer to the five stages of grief—denial, anger, bargaining, depression, and acceptance—which were first introduced by psychiatrist Dr. Elisabeth Kübler-Ross.

Her original project was based on interviews with patients who had received a terminal diagnosis. As she interviewed her subjects, she started to notice a pattern of similarity. Not that all patients experienced all the *stages*, as she would refer to them, and not that they wouldn't experience other emotions, but these five stages of dying showed up regularly. She wrote about her finding in her book *On Death and Dying*.[3] Some researchers have discredited her as being anecdotal in nature rather than scientifically sound.

Regardless of Elisabeth Kübler-Ross's approach, Dr. Ira Byock wrote about the positive influence Dr. Kübler-Ross's work had on the medical community. She said,

> Kübler-Ross and this book (*On Death and Dying*) captured the nation's attention and reverberated through the medical and general cultures. The very act of listening delivered illness and dying from the realm of disease and the restricted province of doctors to the realm of lived experience and the personal domain of individuals.
>
> *On Death and Dying* sparked changes to prevailing assumptions and expectations that transformed clinical practice within a very few years. In reasserting people's personal sovereignty over illness and dying, Kübler-Ross's book brought about a radical restructuring of

patients' relationships with their doctors and other clinicians. Suddenly, how people died mattered.[4]

Dr. Byock further spoke to the linear approach to the stages:

Popularized as Kübler-Ross's "stages of dying," they have been criticized for suggesting a formulaic progression of phases through the dying process. Anyone reading the book will recognize this characterization as a simplistic and inaccurate representation of what she described. In *On Death and Dying*, Kübler-Ross made it clear that these emotional states and adaptive mechanisms occur in a variety of patterns.[5]

In the 40th anniversary edition of *On Death and Dying*, Dr. Allan Kellehear said in his foreword, "*On Death and Dying* was never a study of grief and bereavement. It was a discussion of some key emotional reactions to the experience of the dying. Yes, grief was a part of that experience, but it was not the totality of the experience."[6]

On Death and Dying was originally published in 1969. In 2005, the year after Dr. Kübler-Ross's death in 2004, the book she cowrote with author David Kessler, *On Grief and Grieving*, was published. In this book they outlined how the five stages of dying could be applied to grief.

David Kessler wrote,

The five stages—denial, anger, bargaining, depression, and acceptance—are a part of the framework that makes up our learning to live with the one(s) we lost. They are tools to help us frame and identify what we may be feeling. But they are not stops on some linear time line in grief.

In our book, *On Grief and Grieving*, we present the adapted stages in the much-needed area of grief. The stages have evolved since their introduction and have been very misunderstood over the past four decades. They were never meant to help tuck messy emotions into neat packages. They are responses to loss that many people have, but there is not a typical response to loss as there is no typical loss.[7]

Unfortunately, pop culture has made the five stages of grief not only popular but also thoroughly misunderstood and over simplified. Like in the classic game of telephone where the message is passed down and diluted at best, or completely mangled at worse, we view the five stages as gospel with five linear phases. We ask ourselves, "What stage of grief am I in?" and "How can I move to the next stage?"

We become disoriented when we perceive that we have moved from one stage to the next and back again. We feel we are entitled to be done with that stage, and we don't understand why we are experiencing those emotions again. The authors warn against this interpretation.

As David Kessler said above, there is "no typical response," and yet we continue to judge others and ourselves on an errant interpretation of Dr. Kübler-Ross's work. The good news is that the five stages of grief helped us normalize the many mixed and strong emotions that we experience in loss and grief.

The five stages of grief can be instructive in helping us understand some of the emotions we may face, but in its simplest form, it is not complete. The truth is the stages of grief are not linear and not everyone experiences all the stages outlined. We experience a mix of emotions in grief.

When my grandmother passed away, I felt happy for her, because she was no longer suffering, and I also felt sad that we didn't have her here anymore. However, I never felt denial, anger, bargaining, or depression over her death.

There is no emotion that is invalid in grief. Our emotions are clues to the healing that's ahead and to our specific needs. They are hints to what we need to work on.

Inaccurately, we feel that we must be strong, either for our family or so we can show up in our life exactly as we did before, or so we can stroke our ego that we pulled up our bootstraps and got through this with little to no effect.

In some ways, I was lucky because I was injured in the accident. My injuries were relatively minor for the level of impact of the crash, but it gave me an excuse for a time to really sit with my feelings and my confusion and start to heal.

However, sitting with my emotions was not all I needed. I used to believe that if I just waited it out, the pain would eventually go away. It's a misbelief that is perpetuated by the old saying, "Time heals all wounds." In fact, it is not the time that heals us but what we do with the time that creates an atmosphere for healing.

Grief is painful because it's supposed to be. It's supposed to signal a desire to change and to get the needed help and support. We don't break our leg and sit and pray and hope that time will heal us. No, we act. Pain is supposed to induce action. Just like when I broke my foot. I didn't sit at my apartment and wait for the pain to subside. I paid attention, and I got the care I needed.

People tell me stories of how they ignored their great losses and accompanying grief and immediately reengaged with life without addressing their wounds. They reach out to me after many years of suffering, still in pain, and confused why this approach hasn't worked for them.

Sometimes I hear people imply that if you have faith in God, you won't suffer in loss. This makes me cringe. We would never tell someone who broke their leg to strengthen their faith and go run a marathon the next day. Why do we put expectations on people's time line for healing their broken hearts? Even "Jesus wept."

———

NOTES

1. A. A. Milne, *Winnie-the-Pooh* (New York: Dutton Books for Young Readers [Penguin], 2017).

2. See goodreads.com/quotes/978-whether-you-think-you-can-or-you-think-you-can-t--you-re. Accessed June 1, 2020.

3. Elisabeth Kübler-Ross, *On Death and Dying: 40th Anniversary Edition* (Milton Park, Abingdon, Oxfordshire: Routledge Publishers, 2009).

4. See ekrfoundation.org/5-stages-of-grief/on-death-and-dying/; accessed June 1, 2020. Accessed June 3, 2020.

5. Ibid.

6. Kübler-Ross, *On Death and Dying*.

7. Elisabeth Kübler-Ross and David Kessler, *On Grief and Grieving*, reprint edition (New York: Scribner, 2014).

CHAPTER 13

Fortifying Myself

*You cannot prevent the birds of sorrow from
flying over your head, but you can prevent
them from building nests in your hair.[1]*

—Old Chinese proverb

I believe three things are necessary to rebuild our sense of self and to reengage in life in a meaningful way after a tremendous loss. To deal with the boulder of grief, we must consistently chip away at it to eventually release the supercharged emotions. We must work to increase our strength, and we must seek the necessary support to help us fill in the gaps of our own understanding. In addition to chipping away to release my heavy emotions, I needed to work on my personal strength to face my challenges.

As mentioned before, one of the most dangerous myths about grief is that "time heals all wounds." In the early days of my grief, I wanted to believe this was true. I wanted to lay in bed and wait for the time when my wounds were healed. Many days healing didn't even seem possible, so why not lie in bed and admit defeat? If healing found me while I laid there, well, all the better.

I learned quickly that if things were going to get better, I needed to get better. My efforts were a disconnected smattering of activities to reengage with life. I was not satisfied for long with lying in bed expecting something to change. I made many starts and stops at figuring out how to live my life with my new circumstances. Even though I've chronicled how my efforts felt as if they were not helping, ultimately, I believe that every effort I made was for my greater good.

Each day and week that I attended church, I gained inner strength. Each week that I played tennis and showed up in life, no matter how imperfectly, I increased my personal power. Each day that I helped my boys with their schoolwork, engaged with my family, and worked on my relationship with Ron, I improved my sense of self-worth and expanded my strength. My efforts were never wasted.

When I did experience the miracle of healing, I wasn't starting from zero. I had friends, family, and activities that I loved that helped me build on that miracle.

I'm grateful for my desire and determination to reconnect to the good habits that I had enjoyed before the accident, including physical activity, prayer, going to church, playing the piano, reading, and crafting. I believe that the things we enjoy are clues to what will feed our soul. I believe that God gave me specific gifts and opportunities that would and did feed my soul and helped me to heal.

I love paper crafting. Before the accident, I had built a hobby business around sharing my love of crafting, and I hosted monthly crafting nights at my house. One night a month, a half dozen to a dozen of my friends would gather at my home to create hand-stamped cards that I had designed and prepped for them. Some months it felt stressful to do the prep work, but mostly I loved everything about it. I loved the designing of the projects, the cutting of the paper in bulk, and the setting up the projects and my house for an evening of fun socializing over a shared hobby.

After the accident, crafting became a lifeline. Within a couple of months, I was pulling out my tools again to create. I was not good at sending out the dozens of cards I'd made over the years, but I sure loved creating them, and when I did need a card, I just rifled through my stash for an appropriate greeting. During the summer after the accident, my mom and sister helped me make dozens of thank you cards to send to family and friends who had supported us with acts of service, cards, and gifts.

Later that summer, when we drove to Florida to visit family, I brought crafting supplies with me. I remember sitting at my sister-in-law's table and helping my niece learn to stamp homemade cards. By October, less than six months after the accident, I hosted a craft night at my house again, and I continued that practice for years.

Crafting gave me an outlet. In fact, as suggested in Sara Watson's article "How Grief and Creativity Work Together,"

> "Research shows that experiencing sadness results in a deactivation of the left prefrontal areas of the brain relative to the right prefrontal areas," says Dr. Shelley Carson, a lecturer at Harvard University and author of *Your Creative Brain*. While the left hemisphere specializes in positive emotions like joy and hope, the right hemisphere dispenses emotions like anxiety. Unsurprisingly, the right hemisphere is more active during periods of grief. Here's the hitch: "The main problem during grieving seems to be the relative deactivation of the left hemisphere rather than the over-activation of the right hemisphere,"[2] Carson says. So, even if creativity can help to heal and redirect, people don't always feel like tapping into their creative sides following a loss or trauma.[3]

I'm tremendously grateful for my desire to craft, and I can see now how my creative pursuits helped me to heal. This deactivation of the left brain also explains why simple tasks became such a struggle for me. I could not even remember how to do uncomplicated household tasks, such as organizing paperwork and bills. My filing draw sat dormant for nearly two years.

Interestingly, my creative endeavors, such as crafting, playing the piano, and even playing tennis, required both creativity and organization, and I believe this helped me bridge the gap and slowly fire up my left brain again.

Have you ever listened to a toddler bang on a piano? The instrument holds all the tools for beautiful music, but when a toddler randomly hits keys, it sounds terrible. Good music has structure. There's a beat, rhythm, and system in which the notes are in order and sound good together. But without structure, music isn't music; it's just noises. The same is true in our life. When we create structure in our life, when we bring order to our days, we improve our experience, and our life starts to hum like music instead of random noise.

I've always been a creative person, but I've also always been a person who enjoyed and knew the value of structure. When I was homeschooling my young children, there was always a lot of chaos, and I was always seeking for ways to create structure. For example, we had a starting time for our studies each morning. One morning my aunt called while I was getting ready for my morning. I had put in my right contact and was just preparing to put in the left one when the phone rang. I answered the call and was having a nice chat with my aunt when I saw the time and realized that school started right then. I immediately ended the call and went straight to the living room to start our school day. I didn't put my left contact in until noon that day. I was focused on keeping the structure of our studies.

In my early days of grief, there was little structure, and there's good reason that this was the case. It took me awhile, but over time, I was able to find structure again after the accident. I believe one of the reasons our habits change so drastically after a trauma is that we have turned off our left brain and are functioning in our right brain.

In an article for healthline.com, Ann Pietrangelo explains the differences between the left brain and the right brain. She says,

> The left brain is more verbal, analytical, and orderly than the right brain. It's sometimes called the digital brain. The right brain is more visual and intuitive. It's sometimes referred to as the analog brain. It has a more creative and less organized way of thinking.[4]

In grief we are operating from a less-organized way of thinking. I think this is brilliant! I believe this further demonstrates the human body's unique and inspired design. I imagine our brains trying to assimilate the tremendous changes caused by loss and using all the creative power it can muster. It makes sense to me that our analytical brain would be suppressed as we try to make new and creative connections before we reorganize our existence. I believe it's part of the reason we feel confused, disoriented, and knocked off balance in our grief, but it also allows us to make important connections that otherwise we would be less likely to discover. This understanding also highlights the importance of facing our pain and grief! If we don't work to reorganize and create a new way of thinking and feeling, we may risk staying in this place of chaos and disorder.

It's important to note that the timing for reorganization, for healing, and for fully functioning without the drag of grief is not defined. No one can say how long it will take to heal or what your healing will look or feel like.

Dr. Lisa M. Shulman says,

For people experiencing loss, I believe demystifying the experience is an important step toward healing. When we think about brain trauma, we usually think about physical injury. But we now understand that the emotional trauma of loss has profound effects on the mind, brain, and body.[5]

Further, Shulman advises that

Recovery depends upon gradually reconnecting with suppressed memories—the emotions and memories that we're not ready to face. Disturbing dreams by night and intrusive thoughts by day are evidence of traumatic memories that are buried in the subconscious and were never properly integrated with past memories and emotions, our previous life experience.

To move forward, we need to find tools that will help us reconnect with suppressed memories. Equally important is the need to find activities that are diverting to refresh the mind. Tools for reconnection may include journaling, faith-based practices, meditation, and seeing a counselor.[6]

Self-care is a buzz word, and we all have different reactions to the idea of it. The truth is that taking care of ourselves includes creating some structure around how we fortify our physical, mental, emotional, and spiritual being. As we move through the continuum of grief and healing, we slowly introduce more structure.

The field of positive psychology has determined that the daily practices of recording our gratitude, journaling a positive experience, doing an act of kindness, meditating, and exercising can significantly increase our wellbeing. These positive practices are powerful, although it doesn't preclude the need for grief work. Grief is work. To rebuild, we painstakingly empty the painful overwhelm and we refill our bucket through inspired and positive input. As I worked on purposely adding inspiration and positive activity into my life, I gained strength.

Dr. Dispenza suggests that "the only way we can change our lives is to change our energy—to change the electromagnetic field we are constantly broadcasting. In other words, to change our *state of being*, we have to change how we think and how we feel." And it's worth repeating that he also said, "To be empowered—to be free, to be unlimited, to be creative, to be genius, to be divine—that is who you are. . . . Once you feel this way, memorize this feeling; remember this feeling. This is who you really are."[7]

The need for positive, purposeful input is further supported by research. Our thoughts are powerful, and I try to be more intentional about how I spend my time and what I'm absorbing from my environment.

Dr. Dispenza wrote,

The latest research supports the notion that we have a natural ability to change the brain and body by thought alone, so that it looks biologically like some future event has already happened. Because you can make thought more real than anything else, you can change who you are from brain cell to gene, given the right understanding.[8]

Knowing that our thoughts change our biology is reason to pay attention to our environment that influences our thinking.

Like positive psychology, Dr. Dispenza also recommends meditation that brightens our hope in the future. He says,

Don't make your meditations about that person, thing, or event in the past that holds you prisoner—make it about your future self who is free of their past. Meditation opens the door between the conscious and subconscious minds. We meditate to enter the operating system of the subconscious, where all of those unwanted habits and behaviors reside, and change them to more productive modes to support us in our lives.[9]

Another form of meditation is prayer. As I mentioned, prayer is an important part of my spiritual practices. In his book *Genie in Our Genes*, Dawson Church wrote about the power of prayer.

Prayer is one of the most powerful forms in which intention is packaged. Prayer has been the subject of hundreds of studies, most of which showed that patients who are prayed for get better faster. Larry Dossey, in *Prayer Is Good Medicine*, says that there are over 1,200 scientific studies demonstrating the link between prayer and intention and health and longevity. Meta-analyses in the *Annals of Internal Medicine* and the *Journal of Alternative and Complementary Medicine* have compiled the results of many studies and found that prayer, distant healing, and intentionality have significant effects on healing.[10]

Of course, if you're a praying person, you don't need a study to confirm to you the benefits of prayer. And while this quote appears to refer to physical healing, I believe there are significant similarities to physical and emotional healing.

As I continue to work on my personal development, I have incorporated a habit of morning and evening routines that bookcase my day and include opportunities for continual growth.

Over the years, I have read many books that recommend a morning routine. Each time I came across this concept, I would try to adopt the writers' suggested schedule to resounding failure. My attempts were futile, because I didn't adapt them to my needs and lifestyle. I tried to put a square peg into a round hole.

I understood and agreed with the concept of a morning routine in theory but struggled to find a routine that worked for me. On my very first vision board I created just a few years ago, I put a morning routine in the middle. I desired to adopt this practice and make it work for me. I've done just that, and it looks very different than I imagined it would. In my current self-care practice, each week I review how I'm feeling and what areas of my routine I can focus on to improve the quality of my life.

Over time, I learned four important concepts to establishing a morning routine. First, I needed to start small. When I say small, I mean tiny.

In the beginning, I started with two activities on my list. I added activities like brushing my teeth to my morning checklist. It wasn't that I would forget to brush my teeth if I didn't have it on my list. No, heaven forbid. It was exactly because it was already a habit that I added it to my list to begin with. This got me into the habit of paying attention and using my checklist. I could build from my meager beginnings, but I needed to start somewhere, and starting big was always an epic failure.

Second, I consider what brings me joy. For me, that's music, spiritual practices, using essential oils to boost my mood, taking my supplements, and so on. My list is always evolving. My morning routine was set up to uplift the start of my day. I used to think the purpose of a morning routine was to beat myself into submission. That attitude is probably why it never worked before! Now my routine is not something to dread but something that energizes me and gets me excited to get up in the morning.

Third, I need to track my morning and evening routines. Admittedly, I'm more consistent in tracking my morning routine. Without tracking what I was doing on my routine each day, I never knew how consistent I was being or what was working and what wasn't. Learning to track was why I added brushing my teeth on my first lists. Tracking things I was already successful in doing helped me develop the habit of tracking. I could check it off. Immediate success!

Fourth, I learned that a morning routine does not have to look the same week after week. Each week I review how I did the week before. I try not to review it with judgment but rather with curiosity. If I wasn't consistent, why was I inconsistent? If there was a specific thing I avoided, why did I avoid it? How did my mornings feel? How did my evenings feel? Are there any changes I can make to my routine to improve it for the coming week?

NOTES

1. See goodreads.com/quotes/243520-a-chinese-proverb-reminds-us-you-cannot-prevent-birds-of. Accessed June 1, 2020.

2. Shelley Carson, *Your Creative Brain* (San Francisco: Jossey-Bass, 2012).

3. See headspace.com/blog/2017/04/18/grief-creativity-together/. Accessed June 1, 2020.

4. See "Left Brain vs. Right Brain: What Does This Mean for Me?," healthline.com/health/left-brain-vs-right-brain. Accessed June 1, 2020.

5. Lisa M. Shulman, *Before and After Loss: A Neurologist's Perspective on Loss, Grief, and Our Brain* (Baltimore: Johns Hopkins University Press, 2018).

6. Ibid.

7. Joe Dispenza, *Breaking the Habit of Being Yourself*, reprint edition (Carlsbad, CA: Hay House, 2013).

8. Ibid.

9. Ibid.

10. Dawson Church, *Genie in Our Genes*, second edition (Toronto, ON, Canada: Energy Psychology Press, 2009).

Carrie, Stephanie, and David, 2007

CHAPTER 14

Post-Traumatic Growth

It's true that healing will come with time,
but post-traumatic growth requires insight.[1]

—Dr. Lisa M. Shulman

I believe the forced reorganization of our way of thinking and being is why we have the opportunity to experience overwhelming growth during a time of tremendous pain and trauma.

While I experienced post-traumatic stress disorder, or PTSD, following the accident, I also experienced post-traumatic growth because of the searching, adapting, and struggling associated with my trauma. In fact, if there is a positive in our trials, it's that growth is more likely than an emotional disorder. An athlete stresses their muscles by training in order to gain strength. In much the same way, emotional stress and trauma can have the same effect on building our muscle of emotional strength.

According to a post-traumatic growth article of 2004, "Reports of growth experiences in the aftermath of traumatic events far outnumber reports of psychiatric disorders, since continuing personal distress and growth often coexist."[2]

In 2010, when I felt the darkness depart and the light reenter my being because of God's infinite grace, everything shifted for me. The light brought happiness and rebirth, but there remained a sense that my healing journey wasn't over.

The next year, my husband's job transferred us to Crestwood, Kentucky, a suburb northeast of Louisville. My wonderful tennis and neighborhood friends surprised me with a going-away party. I was heartbroken to leave behind this family that I loved so much, but I was in a much better condition to move than I had been when Ron's work threatened to transfer us to Utah just months after Carrie and David died.

When we got the offer to move to Kentucky, we had just finished a kitchen remodel after completing some other renovations in our house. We were comfortable. But the updates also put us in a great position to sell our home. At the same time, it made it harder to leave a home we had just personalized with our efforts and the assistance of friends and contractors. Overall, the changes definitely gave us a boost as we prepared our home to put it on the market.

In the four years since the accident, I had moved David's things out of the room he shared with his brother and later moved Carrie's things out of her bedroom to reclaim the space for our other children. Eventually our daughter Stephanie and her husband, Chris, moved back to Texas and moved into that room. They even brought their first baby home from the hospital while they lived with us. It just felt so right that the room was set up to receive light, life, and new beginnings.

Even though we had continued to update the spaces, there was still a lot of work to do to sort through our things in our home that we had lived in for almost ten years. During those years I had homeschooled my children. I was a book collector, and I loved curriculum. I was happy to accommodate each child's learning style with new books and materials year after year. Just like Carrie's and David's things, the books held precious memories.

I also had collected a lot of crafting supplies. I enjoyed creating, and I still do, but I knew I had more supplies than I could possibly use in three lifetimes. I knew it was time to bless others with my abundance of homeschooling materials and crafts supplies, so I sold things at pennies on the dollar and I gave away boxes of the excess. The mindset of blessing others with my things is a thought that helps me let go of the things I no longer use, although I still hang onto more than I need.

As I sorted through the closets of memories and let go of boxes of unneeded supplies, I could feel the unburdening of my spirit. It was a cleansing of not only our space but also of my soul. Somehow, I sensed that I had to let go of the past to move into the future, while still remembering the importance of what had brought us to where we were.

I'm not talking about letting go of people. We never let go of people. I will never let go of Carrie and David or my many friends that now live far from us, but I can let go of the pain of separation and bring them into the future with me with love and gratitude.

We prepared our home and it sold immediately. I knew this move would be different than previous moves, but I didn't anticipate how hard it would really be. When we got to Crestwood, I enjoyed the slower pace for a time since I had left behind my obligations in Texas, but I missed my friends. I felt lost and lonely. My children were buried in Texas. Everything I had rebuilt since they died was in Texas.

I could not let go of the thought that no one in Kentucky would ever know Carrie and David. I felt like I buried them all over again. They were still alive in Texas, in our conversations, and in our memories, but in Kentucky, it felt like they didn't exist. I was consumed with thoughts of them and missed them all over again.

I dealt with old demons. At first, I was fearful of going to church. I was uncomfortable, and my husband had to urge me to go. He made friends quickly and tried to engage me too, but I was reluctant. Our church congregation was huge. When I called our new bishop that August to let him know we were moving in, he told me that we were the twenty-sixth family to move in that summer!

If we arrived too late for church, the pews were filled, and we were left out in the foyer for another fifteen minutes while they tried to add more chairs in the back. I felt invisible in a huge sea of unfamiliar faces, and I shrunk into the background.

Even though I struggled, once again God did not leave me alone. Even though I felt insecure, many of the women I met embraced me and invited me to join their circle of friendship.

On one occasion, my friend Theresa and I visited a woman Karen because of a church assignment. Theresa knew us both but never let me know that we shared a common bond. As we visited that day, I opened up quickly about my children's deaths almost five years before. I was surprised I said anything. While I was generally frank about what had happened, I rarely brought it up just after meeting someone for the first time. Then Karen told me that she had also lost two children, the second being a baby who died of crib death. When she told me her story, I once again could feel the intensity of such a tragedy and was filled with compassion. Karen sensed my need for connection, and we became good friends. God knew what I needed, and he provided.

I felt depressed for the first few months I lived in Kentucky, and I had a genuine fear of falling off the edge again. I was terrified. I never wanted to go back to that deep darkness I had felt before. Fortunately, it never progressed that far, but I couldn't avoid how I felt. Even though I experienced a level of depression after the move, I never fell into the utter desolation I had previously felt.

One weekend, Ron and I traveled from Kentucky to Virginia for our nephew's wedding. The wedding was held in an idyllic country setting. The reception was in a beautiful, elevated, and covered open structure in the trees.

We were in Amish country, and a local Amish family had built the structure. Even the meal was prepared and served by the Amish. It should have been a time of happiness and thanksgiving, but again, I felt inadequate and insecure.

As we sat in our assigned seats at dinner, I noticed I was seated next to an attractive stranger. I begged Ron to trade places with me so I didn't have to talk to this woman. He refused, and I was nearly in tears. I felt true fear and panic at the prospect of interacting with a stranger. Again, my fears were unfounded. She was a wonderful dinner companion and we spent a pleasant evening together chatting.

Today, I don't recognize the woman I was then. I can't imagine being so upset about sitting next to someone I don't know. My fears at the time were real and large, even though they were baseless.

In Kentucky, I lived only a little more than three hours from my mom and sister in Nashville. We burned up the roads driving back and forth for visits. That was a highlight of my time there, but I know they struggled to understand why the move was so hard for me. They frequently reminded me that we were so lucky to live so close to each other. They were right, but it didn't and couldn't negate the healing I needed to do.

When we moved to Crestwood, Ron and I signed up for an exercise class with a personal trainer. She was an upbeat instructor who didn't let anything slow her down. A couple of times she talked about losses she'd had and said that she'd only missed a day of her routine because of them. Her philosophy was to just keep moving. To me it felt like she was ignoring her pain, but perhaps I told myself that to avoid feeling deficient all over again. I would learn later that it's not helpful for me to compare how I deal with my losses to how others deal with theirs. We are all different and respond differently.

As painful as it was initially, I'm sure my Heavenly Father was instrumental in all the amazing growth and experiences I had in Kentucky. I had so many successes in Kentucky that were perfectly orchestrated for my benefit. By the end of our stay in Kentucky, I was a stronger, more capable and confident version of myself. I had lived through another layer of healing.

Our son James was the only of our children still at home. He started his junior year of high school the day after we arrived in Crestwood. When he graduated from high school two years later, we learned we were moving back to Texas again.

I'm convinced that the move was for James as much as it was for any of us. He went through some difficult experiences while we were there. Fortunately, loving teachers and leaders surrounded him. They cared for him and helped him through to the other side. There can be no greater blessing than having your children well cared for.

We lived in Kentucky for two years. I have never met so many good people in one place and made so many close friends in such a short period of time. I have amazing memories of the wonderful people that surrounded us there.

Theresa said once of our small country town: "This is a place of healing." She was right. I was surrounded by tremendous friendship, love, and acceptance. I miss my Kentucky friends. I'm grateful to have found a new level of healing while I was there.

When we returned home to Texas, I could feel how much stronger I was. The difference was profound. Moving away from where I had spent so much time raising my kids, struggling with the adjustment, and moving back, proved to be a walk through the refiner's fire, and I could feel the layer of strength I had gained from the experience.

Much like the proverbial chick that must break the layer of shell to immerge into the world, I had to battle my way through my own struggles to become a stronger version of myself. If someone assists the chick as it breaks free from its shell, the chick dies. Why? Because the struggle is the very thing that gives the chick the strength to survive.

As Bryant McGill said, "The number one skill in life is not giving up." I believe this is true. We never stand still. We are either growing or losing ground. When I stopped having patience in my suffering, I lost ground and almost lost the battle. I learned that even in our darkest moments when all we can do is reach for God's hand, we can choose to stretch our arms toward him no matter how weak our reach feels. This is progress.[3]

I spent years looking for answers, but I never gave up. I never stopped believing that the answers were there. I knew the answers existed, and I knew I must continue to search. The answers eventually came, right on time. Not in the timing I would like, but with hindsight, I can see that they came at the perfect time. When we don't give up, the solutions eventually arrive, even when we think they are delayed.

I have been a student of grief for many years now. I've read many, many pages of others' grief journeys, self-help, and spiritual text to help me understand life, death, and grief. I have read many times the importance of being grateful for our trials, but I didn't think that gratitude for the trial of the accident and my children's deaths would ever come. In the past, I had felt gratitude for other tribulations, but this was different.

Dieter F. Uchtdorf said, "Being grateful *in* our circumstances is an act of faith in God. It requires that we trust God and hope for things we may not see but which are true. By being grateful, we follow the example of our beloved Savior, who said, 'Not my will, but thine, be done.' "[4]

I had worked through the agony of my loss to acceptance, but gratitude seemed a trillion miles away and completely unattainable. One day during our move from Kentucky to Texas, while reading yet another book about grief, the gratitude settled on my soul like the dews from heaven, infused with brilliant light. I had been offered a gift, and I accepted the gift of gratitude for all I had endured.

It's not easy to admit that I am grateful for this horrific tragedy. I can feel people arguing with me. How can you be thankful for such a horrendous event? The answer is that I don't fully understand it either. I certainly would love to have my children still here with me. Sometimes I daydream about what my life would be like if they were still here. Carrie would be twenty-three, and David would be twenty-one—young adults in the prime of their life, possibly going to college, starting a career, marrying, and starting families. But they are not here, and I have accepted that they are right where they are meant to be, on the other side of eternity, cheering us on.

I do know that God has blessed me a hundred-fold, and he has more in store for me as I continue to seek higher and higher levels of healing, which I believe are available to everyone without exception. When I ponder the years of struggle and rebuilding, I can't imagine how I could have learned all I've learned without the significant trials of my soul, and for that, I am infinitely grateful.

The long hours of figuring it out, reading, studying and listening, of seeking the wisdom of others in person or vicariously through their writings, of asking Heavenly Father and listening for answers, of living in that space between earth and heaven have blessed my life in significant ways that could never be explained in words.

Letting go of the pain of loss is a process that is often stalled by the idea that if we let go of the pain, we are letting go of the person we love. We have created a bridge of grief to the person and inaccurately feel that the grief is what keeps our love and connection alive. Grief is part of the healing process. It's the feelings we need to experience to assimilate our loss and to adapt to our new circumstances. I believe grief is meant to be a season, not a lifestyle.

No one escapes grief. We all will experience it. If we believe that we must hang onto grief instead of using it as fuel to heal, we will create long-term suffering. When we place grief in its proper place in the healing process, grief can have value and purpose.

Dr. Laura Koniver said,

Grief after experiencing a sudden loss or unexpected change in circumstance can knock your feet right out from under you. But it can also make room for growth. I still remember being in medical school and learning all about the classic model of the grief process, set forth by the amazing and brave Elisabeth Kübler-Ross: DABDA, meaning: D—denial, A—anger, B—bargaining, D—depression, A—acceptance. We learned in med school how patients go through this grieving process in any order and may take as long as necessary in each phase before coming through to acceptance of the loss. But what I found, through both patient experiences and my own first-hand personal experiences, is that this model did not serve me (or my patients) very well. The new paradigm, for me, looks more like this: Resistance ——→ Surrender. Not moving randomly through the five phases of denial, anger, bargaining, depression, and acceptance, but moving systematically from resistance to surrender. Denial feels like: "*This cannot (or should not) be happening.*" And surrender comes in breakthrough moments of: "*This *is* happening and yes, I can do this, I will do this*" and each time we surrender to what is happening, hope immediately returns.[5]

What we resist persists. I have found it helpful to feel what I need to feel until the loss or event no longer has such an emotional impact. Eventually these experiences can open up to evoke good memories and gratitude, not just sadness.

I love the person I am becoming. As gut-wrenching as my trials have been, I don't see how I could be where I am right now without the growth opportunities I've had. Trials and growth opportunities are a couple—they go together. My challenge now is to understand how to learn and grow in peace and joy. I want to choose to find growth through deliberate action, regardless of my circumstances. In that way, I can always be growing in hard times or in good times.

———

NOTES

1. Lisa M. Shulman, *Before and After Loss: A Neurologist's Perspective on Loss, Grief, and Our Brain* (Baltimore: Johns Hopkins University Press, 2018).

2. Reported on Wikipedia, Tedeshi, R. G., & Calhoun, L. G. (2004). *Post-traumatic Growth: Conceptual Foundation and Empirical Evidence.* Philadelphia, PA: Lawrence Erlbaum Associates. Accessed June 2, 2020.

3. See bryantmcgill.com/quotes/number-skill-life-skill-knowing-give/. Accessed June 1, 2020.

4. Dieter F. Uchtdorf, "Grateful in Any Circumstances," *Ensign*, May 2014.

5. See "The Healing Process of Grief," intuition-physician.com/healing-process-grief/. Accessed June 1, 2020.

Carrie, Arches National Park, Utah, 2005

CHAPTER 15

Finding Purpose in My New Life

When I started writing this book, I asked my husband in jest, "Are you nervous that I'm writing this book? Because, if you were writing a book, I'd be nervous."

He shook his head and said, "You already share everything on your podcast. What's the difference?"

Partially he was right. Over the past few years, I've been sharing my story, and more recently in November 2018, I launched a podcast to share what I had already learned and what I was learning about grief and personal development. It was a bold step.

I never expected to be sharing my story or to be so public about my personal struggles as I rebuilt my life after my losses. I'm grateful to see how far I've come and grateful to understand there is so much more for me to learn and do.

I admire those who can share their pain and their gratitude while they are deep in their pain. I have had friends who have generously shared in inspiring ways during their time of sorrow. Or friends who immediately started events or a charity to commemorate their child.

I sometimes judged myself because I couldn't share or show up in that way. I've come to appreciate how different we all are and how different our purposes are. In fact, just because someone has gone through something hard doesn't mean they have to write a book or start a podcast or share in any way.

But I've also learned that it's important to step toward whatever you feel inspired to do. I once heard someone say, "Knowledge without expression equals depression." That didn't make sense to me when I first heard it. Now I understand it to mean that if I feel inspired to do something and I don't move toward it, I will always feel like I'm not doing what I'm called to do.

In 2012, my mother served a church mission in California. She was asked to work in an employment center. She taught and trained, one on one and through seminars, those looking for a job how to conduct a fruitful employment search.

At the end of her service, I flew out to help her drive her car back to Tennessee where she lives. I was only there for one day to help pack the car before we started our road trip. During my brief visit, she was excited to show me where she had been volunteering and to introduce me to those she had been serving with.

She especially wanted me to meet the manager of the center where she had been working, so she arranged for us to meet and go to lunch with her manager, Christy, and Christy's husband. My mother had mentioned to me several times how much Christy reminded her of me.

Christy took us on a tour of the facility, and we visited for a while. I realized how much my husband and I had in common with Christy and her husband Rob. We talked like old friends, comparing our life experiences and sharing about our families.

Afterward, we drove over to a quiet restaurant close by. While we ate lunch, Rob shared some of his most painful life lessons. He had battled with undiagnosed bipolar depression for years that nearly destroyed his family. After his diagnosis and finding a treatment plan that helped him, he spent most of his time helping other men who were contending with depression.

I was impressed with his eagerness to help others as he had been helped. Christy and Rob were good people, with pure, loving countenances, and I was delighted to have met them.

Toward the end of our lunch, my mom mentioned the accident and Carrie and David's tragic deaths. When she did, I felt my heart sink into that place of pain that still sat deeply in my gut even after a few years of healing. I was coming to terms with my loss in significant ways, but I still wasn't comfortable sharing my pain.

Rob, in his compassionate way, wanted to know more. I shared a little of my journey with him as he listened intently.

It was time to go, and as we walked away from our table, Rob caught my arm. As I faced him, he said, "You're supposed to do something with this. I don't know what that looks like, but you're supposed to do something with this."

As he spoke, I felt his words ring deep inside me. I knew what he said was true. I knew his words were inspired. He wasn't just sharing something he thought. He was sharing inspired truth.

Those words stayed with me every day for years: *You're supposed to do something with this.* I knew from that moment forward that I was. It was new truth, and I couldn't deny the feelings I had when those words were spoken.

But what? What does that look like? Where do I even start? I asked these questions of God and myself over and over again. I felt like I was still trying to figure out my life. I still wasn't comfortable sharing what had happened. I still hadn't been able to verbally admit all the shame I had surrounding the accident. I just didn't understand how to put into practice what I knew to be true.

Three years later, after our move back to Texas, I met a massage therapist through a mutual friend. I started to go to her regularly, and as I got to know Karen better, she shared her own tragedy of her young adult son's death.

In profound conversations, we shared with each other our journey, all that we had learned, and how we had been able to find gratitude, meaning, and happiness in our lives again. We talked about all the suffering in the world. We talked about how people can find healing in their lives.

I loved visiting with Karen. She is a kindred spirit.

One day while we were talking, she said, "You're supposed to do something with this." Once again, the truth of her words touched me deeply. Once again, I was reminded of the conviction I had felt three years before.

That conviction had never left, but I was becoming discouraged in my search for concrete answers to how, and I needed another reminder. I told Karen of my earlier awakening when Rob uttered the same inspired words. I disclosed my frustration in discovering what that was supposed to look like.

What is the "something"? How do I help? Where do I go to figure it out? I had even enrolled in college again to study psychology, thinking I would become a licensed therapist, but it didn't feel right at all, and I quickly unenrolled.

On one of my visits with Karen, I told her about my impending move to Salt Lake City, Utah. "Why are you moving there?" she asked.

"Most of our kids have moved west with the grandkids, and we are opening a chiropractic clinic outside of Salt Lake."

Neither my husband nor I are chiropractors, but we have been long-time beneficiaries of chiropractic adjustments, and we love it. We had the opportunity to buy a franchise, and with our kids out west, we decided to move to Salt Lake and open the clinic there.

"Oh good!" she replied. "That will be a perfect setting for you to set up a wellness center and help others."

"Unfortunately, we're opening a franchise, and we won't have the liberty to add services. The franchise dictates the services we offer, and its strictly chiropractic care. That's it."

I could see the disappointment on her face. "This is not what you're supposed to do. Maybe you can open an office next door to the chiropractic office and work out of there."

We were opening in a newer shopping center, and there was an open space next door. "That's an interesting idea," I answered.

I started to imagine opening a wellness center next door. I didn't know what we would offer exactly, but maybe this was the answer to the "something" I was being called to do. Maybe this is how I could help others with their grief.

But that didn't sit well with me either. I could not figure it out, but I knew I was doing the right thing opening the clinic in Salt Lake.

My husband had come to me with the idea for the clinic. We had invested in a different franchise a few years before with a partner, but our partner ran that business. Because of our experience with it, however, we were familiar with franchising, and we wanted something we could own and operate ourselves.

We started to investigate the idea of opening a franchise clinic, and the more we learned, the more appealing it was—although I was still apprehensive. Ron had always been more adventurous than I was.

As we were doing our due diligence, I started praying for confirmation that this was a good move for us. Ron's job was in Texas, and this would be a big move. We continued to explore our options to make it happen.

One Sunday, while I was sitting in a Sunday School class, I remembered how God had guided me years before when I worked for the medical company. I remembered all the miracles I experienced as I was trying to work to provide for my kids. As I reflected on those memories, the Spirit whispered to me, *I helped you before; I'll help you again.* I knew that this was answer I had been praying for.

I wish I could say from that point on that I was wholly confident every step of the way as we moved forward with our plans. But I did have the assurance I needed and that I would rely on going forward.

When Ron and I started the process, he was working for a company out of state, and they didn't have a lot of work for him, so he had time on his hands to do the work of setting up our business. We hadn't decided yet how we were going to structure it, but Ron was taking the lead in the process and asked me from the beginning if I would support him in it. After getting the confirmation I needed, I agreed to a supporting role.

We signed the franchise agreement and went to franchise training in Arizona shortly afterward. From Arizona we flew to Salt Lake City to search for a location for the clinic.

We met up with a commercial retail agent and spent the day looking at potential spaces. The decision was quite easy since there weren't many good options, and Ron started the lease negotiations process with the landlord.

Two months into the process of developing our clinic, Ron changed jobs, and he went from working a few hours a week from home to working twelve-hour days at an office. If we wanted things to progress with our new business, I was going to have to take the lead.

Early one morning, as Ron prepared to leave for work, he woke me up and said, "You're going to have to finalize the lease contract."

"What?" I was shocked and terrified. I had not been involved with the earlier negotiations, so I felt entirely unprepared to pick this up in the middle.

I protested, but Ron said, "This needs to be done today, and I've got to leave for work right now." He told me where the box was with all the paperwork he had collected for the project, and then he left for work.

Through my tears that day, I attempted to get up to speed on the documents and the legal work and made my first phone calls. From that point on, I was the lead on the project, and Ron played the supporting role.

Each day I was determined to just take the next step in finalizing the contract and then starting the build out of the space. I flew to Utah to meet with the landlord and the builder. I was scared a lot, but little by little, I gained more confidence as things progressed.

Eventually, we sold our home in Texas, and I moved to Utah. Ron stayed in Texas for another four months to work while I moved permanently to Texas, finalized the build out of the clinic, moved into a new house, hired doctors, and opened the business—all in less than two months. I felt frequently overwhelmed, and I held on tightly to the words, "I helped you before; I'll help you again." I knew I had God on my side, but it was hard. I cried frequently. I felt out of my element continuously, but I persevered, grateful for the revelation I had received and a system to follow.

I often reflect on the revelatory words, "I helped you before; I'll help you again." When this inspired message came, I was still on the periphery of the clinic development and had no idea I would be solely running the business with Ron's support.

At the time of the inspiration, Ron was still leading the project, and I was in a supporting role. We were still deciding how we would run the business, and we had even discussed Ron quitting his job to devote his full-time effort to the clinic development. Instead, the business became my responsibility overnight. A loving Heavenly Father, who knew I would need his help and strength long before I did, sent me a miracle in the exact words I needed before I even knew I needed them.

I relied heavily on his promised blessing. Many days, as I drove the thirty minutes from my new home to the business each day, I would pour my heart out to him, remembering his words, asking for his help, and depending on miracles, which repeatedly came.

In March 2019, more than four years later, Ron left his full-time job and took over the day-to-day operations of the franchise. From the beginning, we had a goal of opening three clinics, one at a time, which came to fruition in August 2019, almost four years after opening the first clinic. Heavenly Father kept his promise to help us, as he always does.

During my time managing the franchise, I learned a lot. The most important lesson was the new confidence I gained in myself and in my relationship with God. I could write an entire book about the struggles I experienced during those few years. It was hard. I frequently cried at night to my husband about my struggles.

I dealt daily with personal insecurities, fear, selfishness, and resentment, all the while trying to remember and apply the blessing God had sent me. It was a time of working through personal challenges, working through my questions, and gaining tremendous strength.

I'm grateful God is so patient with me. He must have been shaking his head in amusement, just like a parent watching their toddler who is throwing a fit trying to learn something new. I can hear him saying, "Why are you so fearful? I told you I would help, and with my help, you can do anything!" I'm positive he is still amused by my too frequent efforts to do things on my own, which always ends up creating more anxiety for me.

I can see God's blessings every week, but time often gives a beautiful perspective on how he has been in the big picture and the small details of my life. Many of his blessings are easier to identify after the fact when we can see a broader landscape.

I can see how all the stretching experiences I've had since the accident have come together to rebuild my confidence and me. I don't recognize the woman I used to be—the woman who begged to change seats because she was fearful of socializing with someone new, or the woman who didn't want to lead but instead wanted to sneak in and sit on the back row. I'm grateful God has given me a bigger purpose and a bigger vision of who I am and who I can become.

With an eternal perspective, I'm not sure how much it is rebuilding as it is stripping away what I am not to reveal who I really am. When I act with confidence, cheer, and good will, expecting divine inspiration and help, it feels right and good. It's a testament to who we all really are.

When I feel defeated, whiny, and unhappy, I know that I am stepping away from the divine nature we all have inherited from Heavenly Father. Just as we inherit qualities from our earthly parents, we have inherited divine qualities from our Heavenly Parents. The most important lesson is to build my faith in God and rely on his strength and the strength he has given me as his daughter.

After we opened the second clinic in June 2017, I felt increasingly uncomfortable. I had invested so much time and energy into the chiropractic business and I was moving further and further from finding the purpose that sat on my heart from that December day in 2012 when I heard "You are supposed to do something with this."

I wondered why God had inspired me with two tasks in two separate messages. I now believe that he sent me the business to show me what I was capable of. He knew it, but he needed me to know it before he gave me the next steps.

In the fall of 2017, I decided I needed an outside perspective, and I started looking for a coach. During the summer I had hired a friend who was a health coach, and I learned so much about myself. I began to wonder if a life coach could help me figure out my next steps, including how to create more balance in my life and ease the uncomfortable feelings I had.

By chance I met Kathy through a mutual friend. Kathy was a law of attraction coach. I had a limited understanding of what that meant, but as we met, I felt clarity, so I decided to hire her for ten weeks. I couldn't believe how quickly things shifted for me.

She gave me my first lessons on how to discover what I genuinely wanted in my life. She gave me tools to help me along the way. I was shocked to see how my lack of clarity and direction was hurting me and to discover the absolute joy of getting clear about what I really wanted. It was wonderful to gain that level of clarity and understanding.

In my search for purpose, I learned about vision boards, positive affirmations, and setting intentions. I started to practice dreaming again and thinking about what I really wanted in my life. I learned that I shaped my life with my thoughts, feelings, and actions, and I began to understand the connection between those things.

I started to recognize the beauty around me, and I gained an even greater appreciation for my wonderful family. I began to give more weight to my happy feelings than to my unhappy feelings. It's easy for me to spend my days complaining, but when I can focus on the good, life lights up in Technicolor.

Kathy and I started working together in October, and by November, I had an epiphany. This was it! This was what I was looking for! This was the "something" in "you're supposed to do something with this."

I remembered how lost I had felt after my kids died. I remembered how therapy had helped me gain footing but how lost I still felt after therapy, because I wasn't sure what direction to go or how to rebuild my life in a meaningful way. I remembered thinking when the therapist said we were done: *Done? I don't feel done.*

I knew she was right, that I no longer needed therapy, but I didn't know how to rebuild. I started to imagine what it would be like to help people rebuild their lives, and I got excited. I immediately enrolled in a life coach certification program, and over the next several months, I worked on learning to coach others.

Shortly after I finished the certification program, I hired a business coach, who specifically works with life coaches, to help me structure my new business. My ideas and business evolved quickly while I was also running our franchise.

I knew I wanted to work with people who had experienced tremendous loss and who were trying to figure out how to rebuild their life, especially mothers who had lost children. I felt certain I wanted to gain some understanding of grief beyond my own personal experiences with grief.

I had a sense that most people who came to me trying to rebuild would still be working through their grief at some level. My business coach discouraged me from more training, suggesting that I knew what I needed to know. I understand her hesitation since I'm sure she works with many people who avoid launching their business by just spending years in training, but I was determined.

I found an online school that offered a five-week grief-coach training. I was excited to learn more, but as I attended each week, I felt let down by what I was learning. I felt that the information was soft and didn't offer any tools that I could offer my future clients to help them navigate their grief.

I remembered a book I had read a few years before, *The Grief Recovery Handbook*. I also remembered that they offered training. I looked it up and enrolled in a certification class in September.

There were a dozen people in my training group, each there for a different reason, and each personally acquainted with grief. One woman was a blogger who had lost her ten-year-old son to a sudden illness just after she had started her blog. Her blog had become her personal travel through grief, which is not what she had expected to be writing about when she started blogging. She had more and more people asking her for help with their grief, so she decided to do the training.

Another woman was a licensed social worker looking to do this work to expand her offerings. A few people were there to get the training so they could offer the Grief Recovery Method (GRM) to support groups at their churches.

One of the men who was there representing his church shared how he had gone to the support group after his wife died. One of his daughters had found the group and gained so much from it that she suggested her dad join a GRM support group also. He told us how much it had helped him and his daughter as they healed. He shared how another daughter was not willing to participate in the group, and she remained angry and sorrowful, while he and his other daughter were healing. His example inspired me.

The Grief Recovery Method was exactly the training I was looking for. Their program offered tools and a step-by-step process to educate people on grief and the steps to take toward recovery. I loved their philosophy, and I knew how much their information had meant to me in my grief as well. It became a stepping stone to the work I'm doing now.

At this same time, I was also working on launching a podcast. I've always enjoyed public speaking, and I felt that a podcast would give me an opportunity to personally encourage people each week.

During that year, I felt God's hand in what I was doing. He led me along the way. I am amazed at the people I met and the things I learned as I launched the Build a Life after Loss business, website, and podcast in November 2018 with the help of so many family members, friends, and professionals. This was the culmination of years of experiences, promptings, and dedicated work.

I enlisted my friend George, whom I had met my first month in Utah and who had helped me with the marketing for the chiropractic clinics, to help me with branding and my new website. We met one day for him to show me what he had so far. He handed me a folder.

I opened it to the most beautiful logo I could have imagined. In the folder, he had prepared several pages of the logo in print in different layouts and with quotes and pictures. I wanted to burst into tears to have in my hands physical evidence of the dream I had held in my heart. It was a defining moment.

Just before the website and podcast launched, I attended a women in business meeting of the local chamber of commerce. We met in the back room of a pizza restaurant. After we had all gone through the buffet line and were getting settled in our seats, they invited us to introduce ourselves and our business.

Each woman before me stood and gave their business pitch. As I listened, I noticed that a few of the women had mentioned more than one business, explaining that they wore more than one hat.

I was there to promote the clinics and hadn't planned on anything else, but as I listened to others sharing, I had the idea that maybe I should share about the project I was working on.

As my opportunity to speak came closer and closer, I could feel the nervous tension rise in me. I had never made a public announcement about my new business before, but I knew what I needed to do.

I stood up and announced, "You know me as the owner of The Joint Chiropractic in West Jordan and West Valley, but I, like many of you, also wear more than one hat. In the next couple of months, my new business, Build a Life after Loss, will launch to help mothers who have lost children to rebuild their lives."

As I spoke, I heard audible gasps in the room. After the introductions, so many women approached me to tell me about their personal story or a neighbor or a friend who had lost a child or were going through other tragedies. I was surprised and overwhelmed at the immediate confirmation that what I was offering was needed.

Over the next few months, it became evident that I needed to broaden my scope and include all those who had or were experiencing grief and wanted help as they moved forward. Eventually, I developed a new, expanded program to include more tools and principles of healing that could help people in their grief and healing. Again, God seemed to be leading me every step of the way. I could hear him whispering, *This is what I want people to know about healing. Tell the people it is possible to heal.*

In the past, I was always looking for a sign from God to move forward with big projects. The constant voice in my head was, *Who are you to do this?*

I don't think I'm alone. As I work with people, they tell me the same thing. They have an idea or a dream, and immediately self-doubt arises.

We all seem to struggle with self-doubt, no matter who we are or what we've already accomplished. Occasionally, someone will say that I seem to have it all together. It makes me laugh.

What a miracle that the girl who was afraid to sit next to a stranger at a wedding dinner is producing a podcast each week, speaking to groups, and teaching, training, and coaching others. It is a true miracle.

I've learned the things that we enjoy are not only clues to how to feed our soul, but also clues to our purpose. We are unique individuals with unique purposes.

As my friends and clients share their dreams with me, I'm amazed at the variety of wants and wishes. The world is better because someone is inspired to cheer for a neighbor, to dance, to paint, to start a charity, to build houses, to start a local theater, to teach, to open a new business, or to be the best mom they can be. Our unique talents and desires shape our lives and our communities.

When my first husband and I divorced, I was a single mom with three small children, ages six, four, and almost two. I was working for a great company and enjoying the challenge and association there, but I felt like I was just existing.

When I thought about setting goals, I felt stuck. What I really wanted was to have an intact family, to be home with my kids, and to build a wonderful home life for my family. Because I was stuck in the past and didn't think it was legitimate to have specific hopes and dreams, I resisted setting goals for myself.

Because I was learning to rely on the Lord, I was blessed to accomplish a lot during that time, but I wish I could have seen all the potential and opportunities around me instead of solely dwelling on what I had lost. This has been a theme in my life, and I am learning over time to let go of "what was" more thoroughly and quickly.

When my boys graduated from high school and left home, I faced this same visionless dilemma. While I was homeschooling my kids, I always thought that I would continue to support the homeschool community after my kids were grown. But after Carrie and David died, my interest in homeschooling waned, and I realized I needed to find a new purpose.

I do believe there is a time for contemplating what we've lost: it's our mind, body, and spirit's way of adjusting and recalibrating to our new normal. When we don't face our losses and grief head on, we become stuck, because the grief sinks deep into our soul and lodges there. It blocks our ability to see and feel happy again in significant ways. We can't figure out why we just have these glimpses of happiness but no sustained joy.

I've learned that the questions I ask myself can determine the answers I receive. Better questions, better answers. For example, if I ask, "What's wrong with me?" with an accusatory tone, I'm not likely to get helpful answers. In contrast, if I lovingly ask myself, "What's my next best step?" or "What do I need to learn?" and then quietly listen for answers, I am highly likely to receive the next best step or fill gap in my knowledge.

I have often wanted to be able to see the whole picture before I moved forward. I wanted to know exactly how everything was going to work out and how it was going to look on the other side. I now know that it is good to have a vision of what I want in the future, and I understand that each step will be revealed as I choose to move forward.

Just as in the Indiana Jones movie where he steps off the ledge and the step appears, I have to have the faith to just take the first step in the direction I want to go. Usually, the next step doesn't appear until I've taken the first step.

When my children died in 2007, social media wasn't even a familiar term. I joined Facebook a year later, but it was still in its fledgling state. Now, many years later, when someone needs support, they often seek for it on social media.

Unfortunately, since I've been doing this work, I have discovered the black hole of social media support that usually includes thousands of people confirming together that they have to suffer forever and live with grief the rest of their lives. I just don't believe that's true.

Yes, the loss will always be a part of me, and yes, I will experience occasional sadness as I remember the tragedy of Carrie's and David's deaths, but I don't have to carry around grief to taint my every day and to blur the happy memories from their lives.

I have built on my hope, love, and gratitude, and that is the bond between my kids and me, not my grief and pain. I don't want pain to continually distort my beautiful memories of Carrie and David. I also don't want my pain to obscure my opportunities to build wonderful relationships while I still live.

I love all my kids! Carrie's and David's deaths do not make them more or less deserving of my love and attention than any of my other children. Yes, I had to experience grief and pain for a season, but I had to choose to eventually heal and let go of the grief and pain and hold tightly to love and gratitude.

As I do the work of grief coaching and support, I reflect on my journey of healing. I find this work satisfying and immensely rewarding. I often say, "My mission found me and I accepted."

Our family, November 2018

CHAPTER 16

Choosing to Be Happy

Sorrow prepares you for joy. It violently sweeps everything out of your house, so that new joy can find space to enter.[1]

—Rumi

When asked what they want in life, most people say, "I just want to be happy," but when they are asked, "What does that look like?" they answer that they aren't sure.

Happiness is as present and as elusive as air. I believe that it's in the process of becoming who we were always meant to be that we discover our happiness if we are paying attention and we know what to look for. I also believe that a powerful hope that healing is always available to us is critical to being happy.

It is said that "the three components of happiness are something to do, someone to love, and something to look forward to."[2] Even if we have all those things, it's in the attention to the moments of joy that bring us sustained happiness.

As a teenager, I spent time with a young couple from church. They had married in college and then he had finished his masters degree at Harvard before they moved back to Florida where she was from. When I met them, they were past their meager college days and were living in a lovely home. He had a great job, and his wife, Kathy, stayed home with their two small children. Kathy was only a few years older than me, and her life seemed ideal.

A couple of years later, I was visiting from college, and Kathy invited me to tour their new home. They lived in a beautiful neighborhood, in a spacious home. As Kathy showed me around, she talked about how she was grateful for her new home but it wasn't what brought her joy. She pointed to her grand piano in the front room and offered, "I used to think that once I had a grand piano, that would make me happy."

She offered it as a caution not a complaint. She was happy, but she realized that the grand piano was not what made her happy. Things can never do that for us. Happiness is not outside of us but within us.

When I reflect on my days and years before the accident, I can see that I wasn't truly happy. I wasn't *not* happy, but so much more was available to me. I just didn't know how to access it.

I didn't understand happiness. I was always waiting for happiness to show up with the next "thing"—the next opportunity, the next house, the next pay raise, the next accomplishment.

I was sure that happiness would eventually show up like the plentiful ship that we wait for to come in. Happiness never showed up that way. It never rolled in and said, "Here I am! Enjoy!"

On the contrary, happiness lived within me and offered its power to live in more consistent joy despite my circumstances. But I waited instead and never genuinely appreciated what I had. My constant worry and doubt stood in the way of experiencing the happiness that was available to me.

As a child, I was constantly told that I had a bad attitude. "You need to change your attitude!" was the frequent refrain. But I didn't know how to do that.

I didn't understand the connections between my thoughts, feelings, and attitude. I didn't appreciate that I could look at things differently; that I could choose to feel differently.

I believed that my every thought was true and that I didn't have a choice to think differently. I could offer plenty of proof that my thoughts were true. I learned that my thoughts are actually my opinions about the facts and not actually the facts. That's when I learned that my thoughts and opinions can change.

The tragedies of my years unraveled the constructs of my life. The neat structures that I had created, whether good or bad, were suddenly toppled and shattered into a million little pieces.

My losses, especially Carrie's and David's deaths, forced me to reconstruct my life, to rethink everything, to examine my beliefs more closely and to choose what I would keep and what I would discard. At first, I did this unconsciously as the scattered fragments laid at my metaphorical feet demanding attention.

I tried on a piece here and there. I experimented with another piece. Slowly, the pieces started to take structure again. For too long, I didn't like the new structure I built. Too much angst was being used as mortar to hold the pieces together. I didn't want to live with bitterness and remorse. I certainly didn't want that to be the glue of my existence.

Over time, I learned to be more conscious of my thoughts and feelings. I learned that I could deconstruct the beliefs that were holding me back.

One of the biggest shifts I experienced was when I discovered that I didn't need any more proof to believe what I wanted to believe about the accident. I didn't have to believe that God was punishing me. I didn't have to believe that the accident was entirely my fault.

I could instead choose to focus on the overwhelming evidence that God was trying to communicate to me that things happened exactly as they were supposed to, that it was Carrie's and David's time to graduate to heaven, and that this was exactly their path in their eternal progression. I could choose to understand that being their mother even in death was exactly my path in my eternal progression and that God and his Son Jesus Christ hold us in their hands and know exactly what they are doing—there are no mistakes. And I can choose to know that Carrie and David are our guardian angels. I can continue to have a relationship with them even if they aren't here and even if I miss them being here.

When I chose to fully let them go and to believe in God's plan for them and our family, my whole world changed for the better. I began to understand the meaninglessness of worry, concern, and regret. I became more aware of the juxtaposition of fear and faith. I began to understand what happiness really is.

I traveled full circle from the broken shell of a human who sat across from a therapist who told her, "You can choose to be happy," to a continuously striving, mistake-ridden, empowered woman who knows she can "choose to be happy." I strive to choose happiness every day.

A month ago, I excitedly called my mother to share all my exciting news. I had just delivered a couple of presentations that had gone well. I had several speaking engagements scheduled. I had been asked to fill a leadership position in a respected association. The new house we were planning to build was progressing. We had a contract on the house we were selling. Our businesses were flourishing, and I was making significant progress on this book. In substantial ways, everything was falling into place. I was at what felt like the pinnacle of success up to that point.

Within three weeks of that conversation, everything changed drastically. Covid-19 hit our community. All my speaking engagements canceled, and social distancing and the dropping economy adversely affected our businesses. Because of these setbacks, we decided to cancel the contract on the house we were building. The very first week of "the stay home" order, we completed the sale on our house, moved into a small but nice apartment, and realized how unsure we were about our personal and professional future.

Overnight, life radically changed in ways no one could have ever prepared for. We lost our earnest money on the house build, but that was sunk cost. We were no longer willing to put more money into a future house in the shaky economy.

Referring to our canceled contract with the builder, my husband said, "This is an expensive lesson," to which I replied, "What's the lesson? That we should live our life expecting a global pandemic? I don't want to live that way."

He agreed.

But there have been plenty of lessons. I have made lists of ways I want to be more prepared in the future. I have made lists of things that I should have been grateful for but had taken for granted. As I remember to apply what I've learned, the downturn will be a blessing.

With the work I do in grief, I recognized that the pandemic experience was a community grief experience. I became highly sensitive to everyone's heavy feelings of loss and uncertainty, including my own. We were all experiencing grief.

When we moved into our apartment, Ron and I organized everything and were fully moved in within two days. It felt good to be settled but also strangely unsettling, because we no longer had commitments or places to go. We were in what was supposed to be our "in between" space. In between what?

With everything canceled, I felt I had very little to look forward to. I sat in a funk for a week, exploring what I should or could do next. That week felt like a decade.

I knew that what I was feeling was grief. Grief of what I had lost and the loss of the hopes and expectations that no longer felt possible. I knew it was important to sit with those emotions and to acknowledge my hurts. I made a list of the things I'd lost during this time, everything from not building the house and losing financial gains to not being able to go out to dinner with my husband for his birthday.

Organizing my losses brought some relief and allowed me to work through some of the emotions. With a clearer head, I was able to start letting go of the things that were no longer possible and create new dreams and visions for the future. Little by little, my joy, optimism, and excitement started to return.

I've learned that our power to choose is immense. When I stay in the power of choice, I am able to be the creator that I believe everyone is capable of being.

To me, happiness is not having the perfect schedule or the perfect job, looking a certain way, going on the perfect vacations, gaining the respect of the right people, or having just the right possessions.

To me happiness is a deep sense of self-compassion, love, and joy. It's choosing to see the goodness and light all around me, including feeling God's love, being okay with a bad day or week, and not making it mean that my world is coming to an end. It's being consciously aware of how my thoughts and feelings are influencing my experience each day, being able to adjust my attitude when it's not serving me, paying attention to what brings me joy and doing more of it, and having confidence in myself to face whatever comes my way.

When I act with the intention of living in happiness, I create more happiness.

As University of California psychology professor and happiness researcher Sonja Lyubomirsky wrote in her book *The How of Happiness*, "I use the term happiness to refer to the experience of joy, contentment, or positive well-being, combined with a sense that one's life is good, meaningful, and worthwhile."[3]

While it's natural to feel heavy emotions in grief such as depression, and healing has no time line, grief is a season and not a life sentence. I've discovered if I'm willing to go through the pain—no matter how long it takes—and reframe my experience, I can feel happiness and joy no matter my circumstances.

I am just scratching the surface of what is possible in my own journey with happiness. I'm figuring out how to develop more happiness in my life each minute, day, month, and year.

It's exciting to contemplate what the future will hold. I have big dreams. I work hard not to resent the person I was in the past who was often stuck in self-doubt and anxiety. I no longer feel that is useful or productive.

In order to make a better future, I need to work through the pain of the past, let go of old resentments and hurts, and look forward with hope for the future.

I want to live by these words from Thomas S. Monson: "Don't limit yourself and don't let others convince you that you are limited by what you can do. Believe in yourself and then live so as to reach your possibilities. You can achieve what you believe you can. Trust and believe and have faith."[4]

I'm grateful for Carrie and David, our two beautiful, lively, and loving children who have taught me so much. I'm grateful for all my amazing kids—Stephanie, Kristin, Dallin, and James—their spouses, and their children for enriching my life in so many extraordinary ways. I'm grateful for a loving husband, who stood by me in my darkest hours and brings fun into our life.

I am eternally grateful for a loving, omnipotent Heavenly Father who consistently buoys me up in trials and encourages me in joy—my God who always sends miracles in the darkness.

I believe with all my heart that despite our greatest sorrows, life can be wonderful!

My life isn't perfect, and it certainly doesn't look like I expected, but I am learning and growing. And I have created a life that I love, which is full of hope, joy, and purpose.

Life is a miracle. I want to always remember that and honor it for the miracle that it is.

———

NOTES

1. See Goodreads, goodreads.com/quotes/475219-sorrow-prepares-you-for-joy-it-violently-sweeps-everything-out. Accessed June 2, 2020.

2. Attributed to Alexander Chalmers. See en.wikipedia.org/wiki/Alexander_Chalmers. Accessed June 2, 2020.

3. Sonja Lyubomirsky, *The How of Happiness: A New Approach to Getting the Life You Want* (New York: Penguin Books, 2008).

4. Thomas S. Monson, "Living the Abundant Life," First Presidency Message, *Ensign*, Jan. 2012.

Carrie, 2005

David, 2006

About the Author

*J*ulie Cluff is the founder of Build a Life After Loss©, a company dedicated to helping people rebuild their life following a loss. She's the
host of the popular *Build a Life After Loss©* podcast and a frequent radio,
podcast, and television guest. She's a professional grief coach and loves
speaking to audiences about grief and the hope of healing.

Julie and her husband, Ron, and their Maltipoo, Scout, reside in
Lehi, Utah. They have six beautiful children, including two angels and
almost ten grandchildren. She loves traveling with her family, playing
the piano, painting, playing tennis, reading, and living a full life.

Julie believes powerfully in the human spirit and in the ability for
all to rise from the ashes of painful loss. She knows from experience that
everyone can create beauty and build purpose in their life.

Notes & Impressions

Notes & Impressions

Notes & Impressions

Notes & Impressions

Scan to visit

Buildalifeafterloss.com